Weekly Weapons

For times like these

WEEKLY WEAPONS

Copyright © 2020 by Irvin Adonis

All quotations of the scriptures are from the King James Version (KJV) unless otherwise stated.

978 976 9611047

TO:

____

FROM:

____

DATE:

____

Dedication

This is a compendium of selected scriptures and thoughts on God's Holy Word to everyone who has chosen or will choose to be a member of the Firstborn Church of Heaven.

It is an open dedication to every Anglican, Atheist, Baptist, Buddhist, Catholic, Evangelical, Gentile, Hindu, Jehovah's Witness, Jew, Methodist, Moravian, Muslim, Non-denominational, Pentecostal, Presbyterian, Seventh Day Adventist, and every other faith based or non-faith based individual.

It is for everyone that considers themselves a child of the Most High God, the Great I AM, Jehovah, El Shaddia, Eliohim, Our Father and our Creator.

It is for every reader to take a weapon weekly and be strengthened; growing stronger, being healed, being comforted while experiencing a transformation that allows the reader to better define the true purpose in this life.

THESE ARE THE DAYS

These are the days, these are the times

Herald the message, beware of the signs

God wants us to know his word is for sure

Words mete for all, for the rich and for the poor.

His words says to look up when the events you hear

Don's stand and ponder, or cower with fear

Get your life in order, don't stand and wail

Christ is coming, blow the trumpet, do it, without fail.

The earthquakes are many, climate change out of whack,

Heavenly bodies in full display, nothing holding back

Ahead of wars, crimes, and famines, we all must prepare

Storms of trouble, pestilences and plagues, we've nothing cheer

Nation strives against nation, no time to borrow … in lack

Wise up, understand the beginning of sorrow… Christ is coming

back

In times like these

In times like these

Get ready, get steady, nothing to appease

For 'the times' are upon us, yes, times such as these.

By Irvin Adonis ©

As these uncertain days rush upon us with alarming velocity and ferocity, with surprises of a lifetime packed into a few months, persons everywhere and from every walk of life need added support and fuel to cope with and overcome these times. It is imperative that persons gather the necessary tools and weapons to defend and counterattack against the evils of depression and sin that are so prevalent at this time. In a season when the economy is tanking, climate change is reaping havoc and impacting lives all across the globe; when plagues and pestilences that are reordering our livelihoods, as our confidence in healthcare and food security is daily being threatened, our response is in dire need of a response that can match these perilous days. Our offer to persons must be able to combat and build their resilience. It has to be a response that is physical, spiritual and emotional- these times require a converted mind.

A convert is created when one who is fortified with the truth and faith remains unshaken no matter the circumstances. Paul, the apostle, had the speech and earthly authority to persecute followers of Christ, but his conversion only came after light beamed on him and took him off his pedestal. In like manner, there are many today who are riding a high horse thinking that they are in the truth. Christ, again, is shining His light upon such and will cause unsanctified minds to turn to the truth. Christ's intent is for us to fall from preconceived and unfounded positions into His arms of love and truth.

In light of all that is taking place in the world today, the delivery of Weekly Weapons is designed to be a faith builder and a call to wakefulness. There is coming a famine of the word and many who depended on being fed must now seek means where they allow the Holy Spirit to do the feeding though His word. Weekly Weapons are gems to stir interest and guide persons who need extra support and strength in these days of uncertainty.

Each week, there is an appropriate affirmational phrase or sentence directing the reader's attention to remain committed to that week's devotional. As you witness your own personal growth on your spiritual journey, it is the author's prayer that heart transformation and commitment to walking in the way of God would allow you to weather these days wherein we are being sorely tested. If we hold fast and persevere, we shall shine forth as gems ready for eternal glory.

STARTING ANEW

"For this is the covenant that I will make with the house of Israel after those days, saith the Lord; I will put my laws into their mind, and write them in their hearts: and I will be to them a God, and they shall be to me a people:"
Hebrews 8:10 KJV

The way to determine if we are God's people is to assess if we are abiding by God's laws. Just as God wrote the laws on the tables of stone for Moses, just as those laws are recorded in the ark of the heavenly sanctuary, God has written those same commandments on the tables of each heart. Every child of God must follow them. These laws are a part of our character DNA. If any of those laws are broken, be it in ignorance or by deliberate misguided choice, then we are become law breakers, lawless people and sinners in need of a saviour.

The bible tells us that we all have sinned, so we are all in need of a saviour. When we accept Christ's offered covenant, He restores us and considers us, as though we have never sinned or broken any of His laws. However, we are now to stop breaking His laws. We can only stop breaking these laws if we allow Christ to totally possess us.

The question we must now ask ourselves is: Am I willing to accept this gift of restoration and become a new person in Christ? To grow in the knowledge of Christ, we have to commit to diligent study of His word and be honest with ourselves in being obedient to the messages that God would share with us as we study His word. No matter what our past has been, every day that we live is a gift from God. HE is giving us a brand new opportunity for a fresh start.

WEEKLY WEAPON: <u>Start afresh with God</u>.

<u>POWER TEXTS FOR THE WEEK</u>

1. <u>2CHRONICLES 7:14</u>

   If my people, which are called by my name, shall humble themselves, and pray, and seek my face, and turn from their wicked ways; then will I hear from heaven, and will forgive their sin, and will heal their land.

2. <u>JAMES 4:10</u>

   Humble yourselves before the lord, and he will exalt you.

3. <u>PSALMS 40:8</u>

   I delight to do thy will, o my god: yea, thy law *is* within my heart.

4. <u>LUKE 2:11</u>

   For unto you is born this day in the city of David a saviour, which is Christ the lord.

5. <u>1 JOHN 3:4</u>

   Whosoever committeth sin transgresseth also the law: for sin is the transgression of the law.

6. <u>COLOSSIANS 3:10</u>

   And have put on the new *man*, which is renewed in knowledge after the image of him that created him:

LORD, TAKE CONTROL

"Thus saith the Lord, Keep ye judgment, and do justice: for my salvation is near to come, and my righteousness to be revealed. Blessed is the man that doeth this, and the son of man that layeth hold on it; that keepeth the sabbath from polluting it, and keepeth his hand from doing any evil."

Isaiah 56:1-2 KJV

Allowing the Lord to take control requires boldness, honesty and courage. To allow someone else to take charge of our life is not easy for any man or woman who has been taught to take control of his/her own life. Christ requires our total surrender if we are to spend eternity with Him. We would be called upon to do things as Christ says and not as we want. Are we willing to make such surrender?

Observance of the Lord's Sabbath is a sign that announces to the world 'I am determined to be obedient, surrender and follow the example of King Jesus'. The Sabbath is one of the laws that is written in our DNA that we must abide by if we are to walk with Christ. As we await the righteousness of Christ to be revealed, we tend to look for something miraculous to happen, but the righteousness and salvation we look for is to be revealed in us. We will only experience this revelation when Christ is allowed to take full control of us and for that to happen, we have to make ourselves available to Him.

We know that God is a jealous God because he has told us that He is. He has declared himself a day that is to be kept holy unto Him. Christ expects His people to do justice and allow His righteousness be revealed in us, keep the Sabbath from any pollution it and from doing any evil. All this is only possible if we let God take control of our thoughts, our speech, and our actions.

WEEKLY WEAPON: <u>Father, take my wheel.</u>

POWER TEXTS FOR THE WEEK

1. ## PSALMS 89:14

   Justice and judgment *are* the habitation of thy throne: mercy and truth shall go before thy face.

2. ## Micah 6:8

   He hath shewed thee, O man, what *is* good; and what doth the LORD require of thee, but to do justly, and to love mercy, and to walk humbly with thy God?

3. ## ISAIAH 58:13

   If thou turn away thy foot from the sabbath, *from* doing thy pleasure on my holy day; and call the sabbath a delight, the holy of the LORD, honourable; and shalt honour him, not doing thine own ways, nor finding thine own pleasure, nor speaking *thine own* words:

4. ## LUKE 6:5

   And he said unto them, That the Son of man is Lord also of the sabbath.

5. ## HEBREWS 4:12

   For the word of God *is* quick, and powerful, and sharper than any twoedged sword, piercing even to the dividing asunder of soul and spirit, and of the joints and marrow, and *is* a discerner of the thoughts and intents of the heart.

6. ## ISAIAH 66:23

   And it shall come to pass, *that* from one new moon to another, and from one sabbath to another, shall all flesh come to worship before me, saith the LORD.

LEAD ME HOLY SPIRIT

"... be mindful of the words which were spoken before by the holy prophets, and of the commandment of us the apostles of the Lord and Saviour: Knowing this first, that there shall come in the last days scoffers, walking after their own lusts,"

2 Peter 3:2-3 KJV

Mocking, doubting and ridiculing the word of God (scoffing) are not anything new. Satan was the first to do this when he appeared to Eve and questioned her understanding of what God had told, Adam and herself, would be the result should they disobey God's word and eat of the tree of the knowledge of good and evil. Today, we follow the example of the devil when we refuse to follow the leadings of the Holy Spirit and guiding words of the prophets and the apostles, questioning the word of God.

Why do we do this, even when we know what the results will be? It is because we want to have our own way and do our own thing. Things that give us pleasure but cause God pain are the things we question if it is wrong to continue doing those things even when we know what the answer is. The word says this will happen in the last days.

God calls us to be perfect and we question if it is really possible that anyone can be perfect. God tells us to worship on a certain day and we question if the day that God has chosen is really the day. God tells us our bodies are the temple of God and what should and should not be done with his temple and we ask is it really so? We ask who should determine what I do with my body. We refuse to accept that our bodies are not our own but Christ's. So when we ask ourselves these various questions are we being scoffers? Are we asking these questions because we and seeking after our own lusts? Let us examine ourselves today.

WEEKLY WEAPON: <u>I will NEVER doubt God's word.</u>

<u>POWER TEXTS FOR THE WEEK</u>

1. <u>GALATIANS 5:24</u>
And they that are Christ's have crucified the flesh with the affections and lusts.

2. <u>2 TIMOTHY 4:3</u>
For the time will come when they will not endure sound doctrine; but after their own lusts shall they heap to themselves teachers, having itching ears;

3. <u>MATTHEW 12:31</u>
Wherefore I say unto you, All manner of sin and blasphemy shall be forgiven unto men: but the
blasphemy *against* the *Holy* Ghost shall not be forgiven unto men.

4. <u>JUDE 1:18</u>
How that they told you there should be mockers in the last time, who should walk after their own ungodly lusts.

5. <u>ISAIAH 28:22</u>
Now therefore be ye not mockers, lest your bands be made strong: for I have heard from the Lord GOD of hosts a consumption, even determined upon the whole earth.

6. <u>PSALMS 37:37</u>
Mark the perfect *man*, and behold the upright: for the end of *that* man *is* peace.

I WILL PRAISE THE LORD

"Open to me the gates of righteousness: I will go into them, and I will praise the Lord:"
Psalms 118:19 KJV

Many persons feel the emotion of a song or the pleasant words of a preacher and feel that they are praising God. However, this feeling lasts but for the moment that the message is delivered or the song is sung. This emotion does not lead to lasting change; it does not convict the mind to follow all the statues of God's word. It is nothing more than an emotional high that will require a better song or a better massage to arouse that emotion. This is no different from the addictive behaviour of a habitual drug abuser.

When the gates of righteousness are opened it should be that the heart is yearning after everything that Christ requires. It is a deep and abiding hungering and thirsting to do only that which pleases God. When this attitude is achieved no song or message is required to set the mind soaring on things of God. It becomes an abiding state of mind and daily conversion of the life to do as Christ leads; in the same manner Christ himself sought the pleasure of his father. This conversion will allow reformation of the mind and body to study and pray continually. The knowledge that will be sought is just to please God in speech, in dress, in behaviour and in our thoughts.

Let us praise the Lord, for His gates of righteousness are continually open to us. As we follow righteousness, even as Christ is righteous, we will daily display a spotless, blameless character. This can only be possible if we allow ourselves to be filled with the Holy Ghost.

WEEKLY WEAPON: <u>Lord, perfect my praise.</u>

<u>POWER TEXTS FOR THE WEEK</u>

1. <u>PSALM 20:7</u>

   Some *trust* in chariots, and some in horses: but we will remember the name of the LORD our God.

2. <u>PSALMS 18: 3</u>

   I will call upon the LORD, *who is worthy* to be praised: so shall I be saved from mine enemies.

3. <u>PSALM 34:4</u>

   O magnify the LORD with me, and let us exalt his name together.

4. <u>1 JOHN 4:7</u>

   Beloved, let us love one another: for love is of God; and every one that loveth is born of God, and knoweth God.

5. <u>ZEPHANIAH 3:17</u>

   The LORD thy God in the midst of thee *is* mighty; he will save, he will rejoice over thee with joy; he will rest in his love, he will joy over thee with singing.

6. <u>PSALMS 42:1</u>

   As the hart pants after the water brooks, so pants my soul after you, O God.

LORD, I NEED YOUR ANOINTING

"How God anointed Jesus of Nazareth with the Holy Ghost and with power: who went about doing good, and healing all that were oppressed of the devil; for God was with him."

Acts 10:38 KJV

One of the nice quips used to convey to others that 'Hey I am a Christian' is the clever comeback to the question "How are you?' is "I am too anointed to be disappointed." If it was only that easy to claim the anointing of the Father, just speak it into being. It is not that easy, and we should never be lulled into thinking that it is. Christ was prepared from a child to accept the anointing that came down at the time of his baptism. It was at Christ's baptism that God said, "This is my beloved son in whom I am well pleased."

As soon as Christ was anointed, He went about doing good, healing and basically exposing the devil and works of evil. This, then, is the sure test of being anointed. The evidence of doing good and exposing the evil is to experience a godly life. The success of doing good and exposing evil requires lifelong dedication and daily recommitting of self to be led by God and this will lead to persecution, for the word says that "... ALL that would live godly in Christ shall suffer persecution." (2 Timothy 3:12).

Today, we must seek the same anointing of the Holy Ghost. We need the Holy Ghost to overcome the lure of Satan, to increase in wisdom and to do that which is right. Let us pray for the true anointing. Not one where we glibly say we are too anointed to be disappointed, but we must be reassured by the pronouncement of God on our lives that this is my child in whom I am well pleased.

WEEKLY WEAPON: <u>Lord, anoint me to do good.</u>

<u>POWER TEXTS FOR THE WEEK</u>

1. <u>REVELATION 3:18</u>

    I counsel thee to buy of me gold tried in the fire, that thou mayest be rich; and white raiment, that thou mayest be clothed, and *that* the shame of thy nakedness do not appear; and anoint thine eyes with eyesalve, that thou mayest see.

2. <u>PSALMS 23:5</u>

    Thou preparest a table before me in the presence of mine enemies: thou anointest my head with oil; my cup runneth over.

3. <u>HEBREWS 1:9</u>

    Thou hast loved righteousness, and hated iniquity; therefore God, *even* thy God, hath anointed thee with the oil of gladness above thy fellows.

4. <u>PSALMS 20:6</u>

    Now know I that the LORD saveth his anointed; he will hear him from his holy heaven with the saving strength of his right hand.

5. <u>2 TIMOTHY 3:12</u>

    Yea, and all that will live godly in Christ Jesus shall suffer persecution.

6. <u>HEBREWS 13:6</u>

    But to do good and to communicate forget not: for with such sacrifices God is well pleased.

THE LORD'S SABBATH

"But the seventh day is the sabbath of the Lord thy God: in it thou shalt not do any work, thou, nor thy son, nor thy daughter, nor thy manservant, nor thy maidservant, nor thine ox, nor thine ass, nor any of thy cattle, nor thy stranger that is within thy gates; that thy manservant and thy maidservant may rest as well as thou."

Deuteronomy 5:14 KJV

"Speak thou also unto the children of Israel, saying, verily my sabbaths ye shall keep: for it is a sign between me and you throughout your generations; that ye may know that I am the Lord that doth sanctify you."

Exodus 31:13 KJV

The word of God is clear as to which is the Lord's Day. It is the day that He claims as His own and His word tells us how He expects His people to treat His day. We are without excuse for doubting or scoffing at the day He requested. God has told us that the enemy seeks to change times and laws (Daniel 7:25). The Sabbath in the only law in the entire Decalogue that speaks to time, it is the only one that recognises who the creator is and we read that the worship was moved from the Creator to the creature (Romans 1:25).

We know that what Satan seeks the most is worship. It was the ultimate test that Satan presented to Christ. He actually begged Christ to bow down and worship him, and Christ would receive the adoration that owning the world offered (Matthew 4:9-10). Getting persons to worship on a day that man instituted, was triggered by Satan and is equal to false worship in opposition to what God requested.

WEEKLY WEAPON: <u>I shall remain faithful to God's Laws.</u>

<u>POWER TEXTS FOR THE WEEK</u>

1. <u>LUKE 4:16</u>

   And he came to Nazareth, where he had been brought up: and, as his custom was, he went into the synagogue on the sabbath day, and stood up for to read.

2. <u>DEUTERONOMY 5:12</u>

   Keep the sabbath day to sanctify it, as the Lord thy God hath commanded thee.

3. <u>ISAIAH 56:2</u>

   Blessed is the man that doeth this, and the son of man that layeth hold on it; that keepeth the sabbath from polluting it, and keepeth his hand from doing any evil.

4. <u>GENESIS 2:2</u>

   And on the seventh day God ended his work which he had made; and he rested on the seventh day from all his work which he had made.

5. <u>HEBREWS 4:4</u>

   For he spake in a certain place of the seventh day on this wise, And God did rest the seventh day from all his works.

6. <u>EXODUS 16:30</u>

   So the people rested on the seventh day.

THY WAY IS PERFECT

"As for God, his way is perfect; the word of the Lord is tried: he is a buckler to all them that trust in him. God is my strength and power: and he maketh my way perfect."

2 Samuel 22:31, 33 KJV

Many shun the concept that man can be perfect and believe that Christ is the only one that is perfect. Biblically, we have many who are referenced as being perfect. In particular, we can cite Job (Job 1:1). Many who read of Job's life would, no doubt, argue like Job's three friends that he was perfect. However, if God says that this was a perfect man, then we must re-examine any such argument. Christ sees the heart and holds the standard of who is perfect and who is not. Further, since God said that we can be perfect, then we have to, in faith, believe that we can and must be perfect. True perfection is not found in man's standards but in God's.

Since it is God's standards that determine perfection we have to follow His way to be perfect. Enoch, Moses, Elijah, Abraham and all the rest of the cloud of witnesses that surround us give their testimony of how they attained the status of perfection. The thing that they all had in common was that they all followed God's leading; obedience was the common thread, even though all their situations and time on this earth was very different.

God is our strength when we are weak; He is our strong tower, our fortress, our exemplar and sure defence. The beautiful thing is that even if things are not going the way we want; we can be assured that God's way is ALWAYS perfect. Therefore, if we follow Christ, then we can know for certain that our way will be perfect.

WEEKLY WEAPON: I will be perfect in Christ

1. **HEBREWS 6:1**

   Therefore leaving the principles of the doctrine of Christ, let us go on unto perfection; not laying again the foundation of repentance from dead works, and of faith toward God,

2. **1 JOHN 4:17**

   Herein is our love made perfect, that we may have boldness in the day of judgment: because as he is, so are we in this world.

3. **1 PETER 5:10**

   But the God of all grace, who hath called us unto his eternal glory by Christ Jesus, after that ye have suffered a while, make you perfect, stablish, strengthen, settle you.

4. **HEBREWS 13:21**

   Make you perfect in every good work to do his will, working in you that which is well pleasing in his sight, through Jesus Christ; to whom be glory for ever and ever. Amen.

5. **2 TIMOTHY 3:17**

   That the man of God may be perfect, thoroughly furnished unto all good works.

6. **MATTHEW 5:48**

   Be ye therefore perfect, even as your Father which is in heaven is perfect.

THE SECRET PLACE

"He that dwelleth in the secret place of the most High shall abide under the shadow of the Almighty."
Psalms 91:1 KJV

Ever thought what is the secret place of the Most High? The Most High inhabits our hearts, our prayers and our praises. His habitation requires total obedience to all his commands. His shadow over us is His love. No matter what may happen, we must rest in the assurance of His love.

As we trust in God, we must do what He requires. Today, as in times past, He requires us to set aside a particular day for His worship in remembrance of His creation and His salvation. Just as Moses was told "Make me a temple that I may dwell with my people", the same message is given about His Sabbath. God asked Moses to bring His people out of Egypt so that they could worship Him. He wanted the children of Israel to come to a place where He was their centre, away from the distraction of false gods and daily drudgery.

Likewise, He requires a certain mode of behaviour, speech, dress, diet, education, and worship that is heaven influenced and under the guidance and shelter of the Almighty.

Dwelling in that secret place requires us to be constantly abiding under the loving shadow of the Almighty. It is only those that have made His shadow their dwelling place that will be able to withstand the final onslaught of the enemy.

WEEKLY WEAPON: <u>I shall abide only in Christ.</u>

1. <u>AMOS 3:7</u>

    Surely the Lord GOD will do nothing, but he revealeth his secret unto his servants the prophets.

2. <u>DANIEL 2:22</u>

    He revealeth the deep and secret things: he knoweth what is in the darkness, and the light dwelleth with him.

3. <u>JEREMIAH 23:24</u>

    Can any hide himself in secret places that I shall not see him? saith the LORD. Do not I fill heaven and earth? saith the LORD.

4. <u>PSALMS 25:14</u>

    The secret of the LORD is with them that fear him; and he will shew them his covenant.

5. <u>PSALMS 57:1</u>

    Be merciful unto me, O God, be merciful unto me: for my soul trusteth in thee: yea, in the shadow of thy wings will I make my refuge, until these calamities be overpast.

6. <u>JAMES 1:17</u>

    Every good gift and every perfect gift is from above, and cometh down from the Father of lights, with whom is no variableness, neither shadow of turning.

BAPTISM IN CHRIST

"John answered, saying unto them all, I indeed
baptize you with water; but one mightier than I cometh, the
latchet of whose shoes I am not worthy to unloose: he shall
baptize you with the Holy Ghost and with fire:"
Luke 3:16 KJV

Walking with Christ requires continuous growth in the
word. As we grow we move from a simple milk diet to a meat diet.
This analogy overthrows the notion that how we come to the Lord
is how we should remain. Every day we are to grow and move
from being a babe in Christ into maturity.

When a person accepts **Christ** and accepts water baptism
by immersion, this is the culmination of the first step in a new life
in Christ; this process is called "justification". After the process of
justification we must next seek to become sanctified, which is a
daily process including baptism of the Holy Ghost and baptism of
fire. Both are essential processes for God's people to be sealed.

A pastor or elder may perform the public act of water
baptism, signifying that you have accepted Christ's shed blood.
This demonstration is public and witnesses look forward to seeing
behavioural changes that indicate we have met the Saviour. As
growth takes place in the life of the new convert, the result is the
convert becoming sanctified and being baptised again and again by
the Holy Spirit. After baptism of the Holy Ghost and fire occurs,
power is released and the witness of God's gift is demonstrated to
those around. The Light of God shines forth, calling others to itself
and its truth.

WEEKLY WEAPON: <u>Lord baptise me with your Holy Ghost.</u>

<u>POWER TEXTS FOR THE WEEK</u>

1. <u>HEBREWS 5:14</u>

   But strong meat belongeth to them that are of full
   age, *even* those who by reason of use have their senses
   exercised to discern both good and evil.

2. <u>ACTS 12:50</u>

   But I have a baptism to be baptized with; and how am I
   straitened till it be accomplished!

3. <u>JOHN 1:33</u>

   And I knew him not: but he that sent me to baptize with water,
   the same said unto me, Upon whom thou shalt see the Spirit
   descending, and remaining on him, the same is he which
   baptizeth with the Holy Ghost.

4. <u>1 CORINTHIANS 12:13</u>

   For by one Spirit are we all baptized into one body,
   whether *we be* Jews or Gentiles, whether *we be* bond or free;
   and have been all made to drink into one Spirit.

5. <u>ACTS 11:16</u>

   Then remembered I the word of the Lord, how that he said,
   John indeed baptized with water; but ye shall be baptized with
   the Holy Ghost.

6. <u>1 CORINTHIANS 2:13</u>

   Which things also we speak, not in the words which man's
   wisdom teacheth, but which the Holy Ghost teacheth;
   comparing spiritual things with spiritual.

PATIENCE, PRECIOUS FRUIT

"Be patient therefore, brethren, unto the coming of the Lord. Behold, the husbandman waiteth for the precious fruit of the earth, and hath long patience for it, until he receive the early and latter rain. Be ye also patient; stablish your hearts: for the coming of the Lord draweth nigh."
James 5:7-8 KJV.

Even as God awaits His fruit (us), we are called to wait, albeit, not inactively, for the outpouring of His Holy Spirit in our lives. The comforter came to the apostles as they waited on the Lord. Their wait, however, was an active wait. They prayed and fasted continually, and they put aside differences, becoming unified in their purpose. We must wait with prayer & fasting, studying the word of God, and by beholding the mercy and grace of the Lord daily. Being ready to receive the outpouring of the Holy Ghost is imperative at this time, for the day of the Master's return is very near.

God's patience is truly marvellous, as He waits to see His character reflected in His people. Those who are His people must first understand and recognise what is the character of Christ. Christ's character is evident in the word of God – it is first and foremost a law abiding example. He is just, but not judgmental; pure, but not prideful; holy, but not rebellious; selfless, but not self-preserving; obedient, but not self-satisfying. Be wise and full of understanding. We will never receive Christ's character doing our own thing.

We cannot acquire the character of Christ, unless we deliberately accept the leading of the Holy Spirit to change our speech, actions and thoughts. Let us crave the former and latter rain which is the infilling of the Holy Spirit, which will lead us into the way we ought to go.

WEEKLY WEAPON: <u>Come, Holy Spirit, fall afresh on me.</u>

1. <u>PSALMS 25:5</u>

Lead me in thy truth, and teach me: for thou art the God of my salvation; on thee do I wait all the day.

2. <u>PSALMS 27:14</u>

Wait on the LORD: be of good courage, and he shall strengthen thine heart: wait, I say, on the LORD.

3. <u>ROMANS 15:4</u>

For whatsoever things were written aforetime were written for our learning, that we through patience and comfort of the scriptures might have hope.

4. <u>REVELATION 14:12</u>

Here is the patience of the saints: here are they that keep the commandments of God, and the faith of Jesus.

5. <u>1 PETER 2:21</u>

For even hereunto were ye called: because Christ also suffered for us, leaving us an example, that ye should follow his steps:

6. <u>JAMES 5:10</u>

Take, my brethren, the prophets, who have spoken in the name of the Lord, for an example of suffering affliction, and of patience.

RIGHTEOUSNESS

"Brethren, my heart's desire and prayer to God for Israel is that they might be saved. For I bear them record that they have a zeal of God, but not according to knowledge. For they being ignorant of God's righteousness, and going about to establish their own righteousness, have not submitted themselves unto the righteousness of God."
Romans 10:1-3 KJV

Paul acknowledges that there is zeal, without knowledge, that comes from a deep personal experience. Today, let us seek, and submit to the righteousness of God and let us not walk after our own righteousness. If the way we choose to worship, dress, speak, eat etc. does not follow Christ's leading, our zealous righteousness is our own. Let us study the word and follow Christ righteousness.

Many today pride themselves on following their own way. An all-time popular song is one that belts out the lyrics "I did it my way!" While to the world this song is a song that acclaims a person's strength, this is nothing more than an affirmation of everything that is against God's mandate. Righteousness is indeed close to right living but all our righteous acts are nothing in the sight of a holy God. We must submit ourselves to God and allow His pure righteousness to cover us. This is the only way we shall be accepted by God our Father.

No matter how zealous we are about our faith, let us base that zeal in knowing God. To know God is to abide in His word and be obedient to His directions. Abraham showed that he knew God because he feared Him and was obedient to Him, even to the point being ready to sacrifice his son if that was what God required. That is zeal in the right place, and this was accounted to him as righteousness.

WEEKLY WEAPON: <u>God, I ask for your righteousness</u>

<u>POWER TEXTS FOR THE WEEK</u>

1. <u>1 JOHN 3:10</u>

   In this the children of God are manifest, and the children of the devil: whosoever doeth not righteousness is not of God, neither he that loveth not his brother.

2. <u>PSALMS 119:142</u>

   Thy righteousness is an everlasting righteousness, and thy law is the truth.

3. <u>PSALMS 119:172</u>

   My tongue shall speak of thy word: for all thy commandments are righteousness.

4. <u>ISAIAH 45:19</u>

   I have not spoken in secret, in a dark place of the earth: I said not unto the seed of Jacob, Seek ye me in vain: I the LORD speak righteousness, I declare things that are right.

5. <u>ISAIAH 62:2</u>

   And the Gentiles shall see thy righteousness, and all kings thy glory: and thou shalt be called by a new name, which the mouth of the LORD shall name.

6. <u>PROVERBS 12:28</u>

   In the way of righteousness is life: and in the pathway thereof there is no death.

THE LAW

"Thy righteousness is an everlasting righteousness, and thy law is the truth."

Psalms 119:142 KJV

The Psalmist attests to the unchanging nature of God. God's righteousness is the standard we must strive towards and all the elements of His righteousness are on full display in His law (commandments), which cannot be changed. For us to accept Christ's righteousness, we must abide by His laws. The psalmist punctuates this statement with the message that the law is truth. So no matter what men say, there can be no adjustments to truth. Truth is not relative, subjective or objective - it is just what it is. As we hold fast to the truth and encourage everyone to do the same, let us see the deep connection that exists between the everlasting righteousness of Christ and His never changing law of truth.

There are many who go around the world seeking and positing various arguments to discredit the word of God. Surprisingly, even persons of faith take issue with the Bible, doubting aspects of God's word. Persons who partake in these acts are basically anti-Christ and advancing the work of the enemy of God. With the word of God, there are no half-truths. Hence, no law of God can be changed or adjustable by man's persuasions or self-anointed position. The psalmist declares it as everlasting righteousness.

This righteousness is inextricably tied to the law of God, which is the truth. This law is the Ten Commandments in verity.

WEEKLY WEAPON: <u>I choose to be law abiding</u>

<u>POWER TEXTS FOR THE WEEK</u>

1. <u>JOSHUA 1:8</u>

   This book of the law shall not depart out of thy mouth; but thou shalt meditate therein day and night, that thou mayest observe to do according to all that is written therein: for then thou shalt make thy way prosperous, and then thou shalt have good success.

2. <u>PSALMS 19:7</u>

   The law of the LORD is perfect, converting the soul: the testimony of the LORD is sure, making wise the simple.

3. <u>PROVERBS 29:18</u>

   Where there is no vision, the people perish: but he that keepeth the law, happy is he.

4. <u>MATHEW 5:17</u>

   Think not that I am come to destroy the law, or the prophets: I am not come to destroy, but to fulfil.

5. <u>ROMANS 2:13</u>

   (For not the hearers of the law are just before God, but the doers of the law shall be justified.

6. <u>TITUS 3:9</u>

   But avoid foolish questions, and genealogies, and contentions, and strivings about the law; for they are unprofitable and vain.

WORDS OF LIGHT AND LIFE

"The entrance of thy words giveth light; it giveth understanding unto the simple."
Psalms 119:130 KJV

Very often, we assume the only persons who are educated or well-schooled are able to work effectively for God. We ascribe the task of soul winning to pastors, priests and other church leaders. This is so far from the truth. Christ has shown time after time that he is able to take the simple, unlearned and unschooled individual and use them to confound the learned. The thing that makes the difference is the acceptance and understanding of word of God.

To be a blessing, we need to believe the word of God to make the difference. Understanding is a gift of the Holy Spirit. Many church leaders just see their role as a job or as a position of influence and do not view it as a calling or vocation, thus they cannot be effective in soul winning. Christ's criteria for workers stems from a heart that is willing and obedient. Thus, you and I can easily fill the role. All we have to do is to avail ourselves and the Holy Spirit will transform us to do the will of the Father.

Christ requires a willing heart and one who is ready to engage in deep study of the word to be used by God. The word is the light and the Holy Spirit will provide the understanding.

WEEKLY WEAPON: <u>I avail my life to the Holy Spirit</u>

1. **1 JOHN 1:7**

   But if we walk in the light, as he is in the light, we have fellowship one with another, and the blood of Jesus Christ his Son cleanseth us from all sin.

2. **1 JOHN 2:9**

   He that saith he is in the light, and hateth his brother, is in darkness even until now.

3. **ISAIAH 8:20**

   To the law and to the testimony: if they speak not according to this word, it is because there is no light in them.

4. **PROVERBS 16:22**

   Understanding is a wellspring of life unto him that hath it: but the instruction of fools is folly.

5. **1 JOHN 5:20**

   And we know that the Son of God is come, and hath given us an understanding, that we may know him that is true, and we are in him that is true, even in his Son Jesus Christ. This is the true God, and eternal life.

6. **ISAIAH 29: 24**

   They also that erred in spirit shall come to understanding, and they that murmured shall learn doctrine.

SIN AND ERROR

"Brethren, if any of you do err from the truth, and one convert him; Let him know, that he which converteth the sinner from the error of his way shall save a soul from death, and shall hide a multitude of sins."
James 5:19-20 KJV

To err from the truth is to sin. The Word says we have all sinned and fallen short of the glory of God. Indeed we have all erred, but praise God there is the opportunity for conversion! To be thus converted means that a soul has been saved from eternal death.

There should be an abiding desire within us to try and save our souls and those of others. To err from truth is to step away from Christ. The word of God is truth, the life of Christ is truth, and the law of the Lord is truth; stepping away from any of these aspects of truth means that we err. At some point and time, we all have erred and were dependent on someone to point out our error and thereby partake in our conversion. Upon recognising the errors of our ways, it is our duty to turn back to the word, to the model Christ has shown us and allow our lives to obey the law of God. It is then that our souls will be saved. A soul that is saved and walks in obedience will not face eternal death, for our multitude of sins would be covered, this is the promise of God.

Let us seek to be converted today by seeking and following truth (Christ) and leaving errors (man's teachings and traditions). Christ is truth. Let us follow ALL of His examples and we shall be converted. 'Look upon Jesus sinless is He'. Let that be our commitment today.

WEEKLY WEAPON: <u>I shall abide in truth</u>

1. **ROMANS 5:12** Wherefore, as by one man sin entered into the world, and death by sin; and so death passed upon all men, for that all have sinned:

2. **ROMANS 3:23** For all have sinned, and come short of the glory of God;

3. **EPHESIANS 4:31** Wherefore lay apart all filthiness and superfluity of naughtiness, and receive with meekness the engrafted word, which is able to save your souls.

4. **1 JOHN 2:1** My little children, these things write I unto you, that ye sin not. And if any man sin, we have an advocate with the Father, Jesus Christ the righteous:

5. **Matthew 22:29** Jesus answered and said unto them, Ye do err, not knowing the scriptures, nor the power of God.

6. **Hebrews 5:9** And being made perfect, he became the author of eternal salvation unto all them that obey him;

WHAT CAN WASH AWAY MY SIN?

"If we say that we have fellowship with him, and walk in darkness, we lie, and do not the truth: But if we walk in the light, as he is in the light, we have fellowship one with another, and the blood of Jesus Christ his Son cleanseth us from all sin."

1 John 1:6-7 KJV

God's word is clear, we can't say we have fellowship with Him while we are walking in darkness (sin), doing our 'own thing'.

We have got to depart from every sin to have fellowship with Christ. Christ's earthly example shows us how we are to walk with him. If we follow His example, we shall have fellowship with Him. We can't follow our own way and think to have fellowship with Him.

Many times we examine our actions and think that we are walking in the light of God, but are we really? Every time we refuse to do as God's word instructs, we are choosing to walk in darkness rather than light, and this is how we know that the truth is not in us. One of the principal reasons for Christ coming as a man and living a sinless life is to demonstrate to us how it is possible to walk in the light. The other reason for Christ's coming, death and resurrection was to allow His blood to cleanse all the sins that we have committed. It is the double insurance method that Christ has given so that none should be lost. Sadly, we either refuse to accept His shed blood to cover our sins or we refuse to walk in the light that He has shown.

Let us live and worship as He did to be in truth and have fellowship with Him and accept His blood.

WEEKLY WEAPON: <u>Lord, I accept your blood and light</u>

1. <u>EPHESIANS 5:11</u>

And have no fellowship with the unfruitful works of darkness, but rather reprove them.

2. <u>EPHESIANS 5:26</u>

That he might sanctify and cleanse it with the washing of water by the word,

3. <u>PSALMS 119:9</u>

Wherewithal shall a young man cleanse his way? by taking heed thereto according to thy word.

4. <u>2 CORINTHIANS 7:1</u>

Having therefore these promises, dearly beloved, let us cleanse ourselves from all filthiness of the flesh and spirit, perfecting holiness in the fear of God.

5. <u>1 JOHN 1:9</u>

If we confess our sins, he is faithful and just to forgive us our sins, and to cleanse us from all unrighteousness.

6. <u>HEBREWS 9:22</u>

And almost all things are by the law purged with blood; and without shedding of blood is no remission.

TRIAL OF FIRE

"And I will bring the third part through the fire, and will refine them as silver is refined, and will try them as gold is tried: they shall call on my name, and I will hear them: I will say, It is my people: and they shall say, The Lord is my God."

Zechariah 13:9 KJV

Are we ready to go through the fire that will try us and ready us for eternity? Let us pray for the Holy Spirit to fill us for it is only this filling will prepare us to go through the fire.

We have to ready our minds and our bodies to go through such fire. Gold is not purified by a regular kitchen fire. It is an immense and sustained heating process that purifies the gold. While water is boiled at 100^0 C, gold requires over $1,000^0$ C to melt, so you can then remove the impurities. The only way we can endure the increased temperature to be refined is if we are ready to sacrifice our all. Are we willing to lay down our lives to be purified? The Disciples of Christ had to go through the refiner's fire and so did the prophets. God is just. He will not allow those before us to go through so much and only require of us to say the name of Jesus and be saved.

The scripture says we will call on His name, for it is only in calling on Him and asking His intervention that we will be able to endure the refiner's fire. He is the refiner and will allow no harm to come upon His own. We cannot rely on the world's goods or man's customs to get us through the fire.

WEEKLY WEAPON: <u>God, keep me safe in the fire</u>

1. **1 PETER 1:7**

    That the trial of your faith, being much more precious than of gold that perisheth, though it be tried with fire, might be found unto praise and honour and glory at the appearing of Jesus Christ:

2. **1PETER 4:12**

    Beloved, think it not strange concerning the fiery trial which is to try you, as though some strange thing happened unto you:

3. **ROMANS 5:3**

    And not only so, but we glory in tribulations also: knowing that tribulation worketh patience;

4. **ISAIAH 48:10**

    Behold, I have refined thee, but not with silver; I have chosen thee in the furnace of affliction.

5. **JAMES 1:12**

    Blessed is the man that endureth temptation: for when he is tried, he shall receive the crown of life, which the Lord hath promised to them that love him.

6. **DANIEL 12:10**

    Many shall be purified, and made white, and tried; but the wicked shall do wickedly: and none of the wicked shall understand; but the wise shall understand.

STRANGE APPAREL

"And it shall come to pass in the day of the Lord's sacrifice, that I will punish the princes, and the king's children, and all such as are clothed with strange apparel." "Seek ye the Lord, all ye meek of the earth, which have wrought his judgment; seek righteousness, seek meekness: it may be ye shall be hid in the day of the Lord's anger."

Zephaniah 1:8 KJV Zephaniah 2:3 KJV

What is the "strange apparel"? This is self-righteousness and false worship. In meekness, let us seek Christ's righteousness, for only His righteousness will save us. Let us do so today before the great day of the Lord, or before we die. Today, if we hear the voice of the Lord, let us not harden our hearts.

The story is told of the guest who came to the wedding feast dressed in apparel different from what was required and, was, as a result, put out, bound and banished to outer darkness (Matthew 22). This guest was a friend; he had time to get the correct dress but he chose to turn up at the wedding in his own garb. He was not only asked to leave but he was bound so he had no more opportunity to go and get changed. The time for changing into the right apparel is now, before we enter the wedding feast.

Many argue that their worship style and what they do is a matter between them and God and He would understand their situation. This is true, but God has spoken in His word of His requirements and if we don't measure up, He will have no other recourse but to put us out. He tells us what day we ought to remember as His special day. He tells us He wants us to overcome every sin. Let us not deny ourselves of getting the right apparel.

WEEKLY WEAPON: <u>I shall wear the right apparel.</u>

1. PSALMS 144:11

Rid me, and deliver me from the hand of strange children, whose mouth speaketh vanity, and their right hand is a right hand of falsehood:

2. PROVERBS 21:8

The way of man is froward and strange: but as for the pure, his work is right.

3. JEREMIAH 2:21

Yet I had planted thee a noble vine, wholly a right seed: how then art thou turned into the degenerate plant of a strange vine unto me?

4. HOSEA 8:12

I have written to him the great things of my law, but they were counted as a strange thing.

5. REVELATION 7:14

And I said unto him, Sir, thou knowest. And he said to me, These are they which came out of great tribulation, and have washed their robes, and made them white in the blood of the Lamb.

6. JEREMIAH 13:25

This is thy lot, the portion of thy measures from me, saith the LORD; because thou hast forgotten me, and trusted in falsehood.

RECEIVE YE POWER

"Be it known unto you all, and to all the people of Israel, that by the name of Jesus Christ of Nazareth, whom ye crucified, whom God raised from the dead, even by him doth this man stand here before you whole. Neither is there salvation in any other: for there is none other name under heaven given among men, whereby we must be saved."
Acts 4:10, 12 KJV

Peter and the apostles were granted power from God after they had humbled themselves, repented of their sins to God and confessed their faults to one another. They then waited, hungering and thirsting after righteousness. It was then that they were ready to experience revival and reformation. They were baptized with the Holy Spirit and they emerged with power to speak and do the will of the Father. This is the blueprint for us to follow today if we desire to have that power.

Christ avails his power to all. Some, however, will accept the challenge to seize this power on God's terms while others will criticize those that are seeking that power because they want the same power but on their terms. Those who seek power on their terms are easy prey for the enemy of God. Holy Ghost power is for the glory of God and it is to allow those who are unbelievers to come to the full knowledge of the power of a mighty God.

This dynamic power is to bring salvation to those who seek salvation. The name of the Lord is power; it is a strong tower that the righteous must run into to be saved. There is no other way that man can be saved but through the precious name of Jesus. Understanding the connection between the tower and name can only be understood from dwelling in the scriptures.

WEEKLY WEAPON: <u>I will wait upon the Lord.</u>

<u>POWER TEXTS FOR THE WEEK</u>

1. <u>1 THESSALONIANS 1:5</u>

For our gospel came not unto you in word only, but also in power, and in the Holy Ghost, and in much assurance; as ye know what manner of men we were among you for your sake.

2. <u>2 TIMOTHY 1:8</u>

Be not thou therefore ashamed of the testimony of our Lord, nor of me his prisoner: but be thou partaker of the afflictions of the gospel according to the power of God;

3. <u>EPHESIANS 6:10</u>

Finally, my brethren, be strong in the Lord, and in the power of his might.

4. <u>MATTHEW 28:18</u>

And Jesus came and spake unto them, saying, All power is given unto me in heaven and in earth.

5. <u>2 PETER 1:3</u>

According as his divine power hath given unto us all things that pertain unto life and godliness, through the knowledge of him that hath called us to glory and virtue:

6. <u>LUKE 24:49</u>

And, behold, I send the promise of my Father upon you: but tarry ye in the city of Jerusalem, until ye be endued with power from on high.

EXCELLENCE IN CHRIST

"And this I pray, that your love may abound yet more and more in knowledge and in all judgment; That ye may approve things that are excellent; that ye may be sincere and without offence till the day of Christ; Being filled with the fruits of righteousness, which are by Jesus Christ, unto the glory and praise of God."
Philippians 1:9-11 KJV

This prayer should be the sincere prayer of every follower of Christ for every member of the family, every friend, and every neighbour. It must be the prayer of everyone who is earnestly seeking the conversion souls who understands that Christ has given His life for on the cross of Calvary for every one of us.

We must pray for growth and knowledge on all aspects of the loving Christ whose laws govern His children and their future. Pray for excellence in every endeavour, be it great or small and that those endeavours are in no way, shape or form offensive to Christ; they must seek only to bring honour, glory and praise to His name.

We can only be excellent if we allow Christ to permeate our entire being. Our speech must be excellent; our dress must be excellent, our worship must be in excellence, just as we seek to have an excellent diet which results in excellent health. The word of God wishes above all that we prosper and be in health even as our souls prosper. Our God seeks to give us only that which is best and his best is rooted in excellence.

WEEKLY WEAPON: <u>I promise to live excellently</u>

<u>POWER TEXTS FOR THE WEEK</u>

1. <u>PROVERBS 12:26</u>

The righteous is more excellent than his neighbour: but the way of the wicked seduceth them.

2. <u>JOB 37:23</u>

Touching the Almighty, we cannot find him out: he is excellent in power, and in judgment, and in plenty of justice: he will not afflict.

3. <u>PHILIPPIANS 3:8</u>

Yea doubtless, and I count all things but loss for the excellency of the knowledge of Christ Jesus my Lord: for whom I have suffered the loss of all things, and do count them but dung, that I may win Christ,

4. <u>ECCLESIASTES 7:12</u>

For wisdom is a defence, and money is a defence: but the excellency of knowledge is, that wisdom giveth life to them that have it.

5. <u>2 CORINTHIANS 4:7</u>

But we have this treasure in earthen vessels, that the excellency of the power may be of God, and not of us.

6. <u>HABAKKUK 2:14</u>

For the earth shall be filled with the knowledge of the glory of the LORD, as the waters cover the sea.

CHRIST'S CUSTOMS VS. MAN'S TRADITIONS

"And he came to Nazareth, where he had been brought up: and, as his custom was, he went into the synagogue on the sabbath day, and stood up for to read. To preach the acceptable year of the Lord."
Luke 4:16, 19 KJV

Christ's custom was to follow the unchanging word of God. His message of the acceptable year is the everlasting gospel and the testimony of Jesus which speaks to the soon return of the Lord to take His obedient sheep to be with Him. The word of God clearly demonstrates that Christ followed every one of the Ten Commandments.

We are expected to follow his examples and we know that persons who deliberately choose to disobey any one of those commandments do themselves an injustice by blocking themselves out of spending an eternity with Christ. The only customs we are encouraged to follow are those followed by Christ. Sadly, many believers feel they are being obedient by following the customs and traditions of man rather than the customs of Christ.

Today, let us give thanks that Jesus has given us the message and the pattern whereby we can follow Him into the Father's glory.

WEEKLY WEAPON: <u>I will follow Christ's customs</u>.

<u>POWER TEXTS FOR THE WEEK</u>

1. <u>1 PETER 1:18</u>

   Forasmuch as ye know that ye were not redeemed with corruptible things, as silver and gold, from your vain conversation received by tradition from your fathers;

2. <u>COLOSSIANS 2:8</u>

   Beware lest any man spoil you through philosophy and vain deceit, after the tradition of men, after the rudiments of the world, and not after Christ.

3. <u>MARK 7:8</u>

   For laying aside the commandment of God, ye hold the tradition of men, as the washing of pots and cups: and many other such like things ye do.

4. <u>MATTHEW 15:3</u>

   But he answered and said unto them, Why do ye also transgress the commandment of God by your tradition?

5. <u>LEVITICUS 18:30</u>

   Therefore shall ye keep mine ordinance, that ye commit not any one of these abominable customs, which were committed before you, and that ye defile not yourselves therein: I am the LORD your God.

6. <u>JEREMIAH 10:3</u>

   For the customs of the people are vain: for one cutteth a tree out of the forest, the work of the hands of the workman, with the axe.

SURRENDERING OUR WILL

"For this is the will of God, even your sanctification, that ye should abstain from fornication: That no man go beyond and defraud his brother in any matter: because that the Lord is the avenger of all such, as we also have forewarned you and testified. For God hath not called us unto uncleanness, but unto holiness. And that ye study to be quiet, and to do your own business, and to work with your own hands, as we commanded you;"
1 Thessalonians 4:3, 6-7, 11 KJV

Very often we pray and ask God to let us know what His will is for us. His word tells us what His will is quite plainly. However, in truth and in fact we don't really want to know because when we read in His word and understand what that will is, we then argue that those messages are not for us or it is outdated or nailed to the cross. Obedience has always been an important aspect for God. Obedience is better than sacrifice (1 Samuel 15:22).

We must study God's word and know what He means by 'living in holiness.' We ought never to be unsure of what God's will is for our lives if we are abiding in God's will. When we pray, we can know for sure how He will answer for we are shown what His will is, as recorded in His word. Therefore we must become conversant with His word that we might walk in His will.

The fact that we are told to work with our own hands and do our own business implies that our understanding of the Bible should not be controlled by a church leader or by denominational creeds, but we must seek out the word of God for ourselves and make decisions based only upon His word. While we should study with others as iron sharpens iron, ultimately the final decision is ours and should be based and guided by the word of God.

WEEKLY WEAPON: <u>I surrender my will to God alone.</u>

1. **HEBREWS 12:14**

   Follow peace with all men, and holiness, without which no man shall see the Lord:

2. **PSALMS 29:2**

   Give unto the LORD the glory due unto his name; worship the LORD in the beauty of holiness.

3. **ZECHARIAH 14:21**

   Yea, every pot in Jerusalem and in Judah shall be holiness unto the LORD of hosts: and all they that sacrifice shall come and take of them, and seethe therein: and in that day there shall be no more the Canaanite in the house of the LORD of hosts.

4. **2 THESSALONIANS 2:13**

   But we are bound to give thanks alway to God for you, brethren beloved of the Lord, because God hath from the beginning chosen you to salvation through sanctification of the Spirit and belief of the truth:

5. **JOHN 17:17**

   Sanctify them through thy truth: thy word is truth.

6. **LEVITICUS 20:7**

   Sanctify yourselves therefore, and be ye holy: for I am the LORD your God.

WITHOUT AN EXCUSE

"For the invisible things of him from the creation of the world are clearly seen, being understood by the things that are made, even his eternal power and Godhead; so that they are without excuse: Because that, when they knew God, they glorified him not as God, neither were thankful; but became vain in their imaginations, and their foolish heart was darkened. Professing themselves to be wise, they became fools,"

Romans 1:20-22 KJV

We are without excuse on the things that God requires of us, for we have been given enough evidence to make the right decision. In vain we flaunt our knowledge and intellect, but doing so in the view of the all-knowing, and all powerful God we have become as foolish just as the Pharisees and Scribes of old.

Even if we are unclear about every tiny aspect of the bible we can't refute the intelligent design around us, letting us know that there is a Supreme Power behind the things we see, hear and touch. Mankind, with all the enhanced knowledge and technology, cannot explain all that is evident around us. We are unable to fully understand the expanse of our universe, yet we believe it is real. The word of God tells us all that science is seeking to prove. When the word of God says that we will all have to give an account and we would be without an excuse, let us not reject this truth.

Dear Lord, forgive us and help us through the infilling of the Holy Spirit to confess our sins and repent of them.

WEEKLY WEAPON: <u>Lord, I will not be a fool.</u>

1. LUKE 14:18

And they all with one consent began to make excuse. The first said unto him, I have bought a piece of ground, and I must needs go and see it: I pray thee have me excused.

2. ROMANS 2:15

Which shew the work of the law written in their hearts, their conscience also bearing witness, and their thoughts the mean while accusing or else excusing one another;)

3. 2 PETER 2:2

And many shall follow their pernicious ways; by reason of whom the way of truth shall be evil spoken of.

4. ECCLESIASTES 7:25

I applied mine heart to know, and to search, and to seek out wisdom, and the reason of things, and to know the wickedness of folly, even of foolishness and madness:

5. ISAIAH 1:18

Come now, and let us reason together, saith the LORD: though your sins be as scarlet, they shall be as white as snow; though they be red like crimson, they shall be as wool.

6. JOB 28:28

And unto man he said, Behold, the fear of the Lord, that is wisdom; and to depart from evil is understanding.

WAY OF ESCAPE

"Watch ye therefore, and pray always, that ye may be accounted worthy to escape all these things that shall come to pass, and to stand before the Son of man."
Luke 21:36 KJV

Jesus explained to his disciples all the various signs that would come to pass in the last days (pestilence, heavenly wonders, earthquakes, food shortages etc. all in different places) and He tells us how to escape it. He tells us to move out of the cities and not to become involved in the cares of this life.

He exhorts us to watch (look for the signs and link it to the times) and pray without ceasing. This is what we must do to keep our minds stayed on Christ and escape from temptations. We are not to be distracted by the issues that will arise and seek to draw us into pointless conflicts that take our minds away from being ready for our Lord's soon return.

We need to see the issues for what they are - signs that foretell that Christ is at the door. We need not become embroiled in the issues of this life and feel the need to fix things. The word of God cautions us that this is not what we ought to be doing. We must separate ourselves from the politics, economies and social issues, even as we witness to all men, of the need to do similarly and draw their attention to the importance of getting ready to meet our Lord. The words for today are WATCH, PRAY, WITNESS and BE READY.

WEEKLY WEAPON: <u>I will wait upon the Lord</u>

<u>POWER TEXTS FOR THE WEEK</u>

1. <u>HEBREWS 12:25</u>

See that ye refuse not him that speaketh. For if they escaped not who refused him that spake on earth, much more shall not we escape, if we turn away from him that speaketh from heaven:

2. <u>1 CORINTHIANS 10:13</u>

There hath no temptation taken you but such as is common to man: but God is faithful, who will not suffer you to be tempted above that ye are able; but will with the temptation also make a way to escape, that ye may be able to bear it.

3. <u>PSALMS 91:10</u>

There shall no evil befall thee, neither shall any plague come nigh thy dwelling.

4. <u>JEREMIAH 8:7</u>

Yea, the stork in the heaven knoweth her appointed times; and the turtle and the crane and the swallow observe the time of their coming; but my people know not the judgment of the LORD.

5. <u>JAMES 5:8</u>

Be ye also patient; stablish your hearts: for the coming of the Lord draweth nigh.

6. <u>MATTHEW 24:30</u>

And then shall appear the sign of the Son of man in heaven: and then shall all the tribes of the earth mourn, and they shall see the Son of man coming in the clouds of heaven with power and great glory.

FAMINE IN THE LAND

"Behold, the days come, saith the Lord God, that I will send a famine in the land, not a famine of bread, nor a thirst for water, but of hearing the words of the Lord:"
Amos 8:11 KJV

Today this word is being fulfilled. As restrictions to assemble are being put in place we recognize the pangs of a famine. It is not only a famine of bread but especially a famine of the hearing the words of the Lord. Christ has been speaking and we have not been storing. Instead we have been resisting and refusing to obey His words.

Paul, the apostle, had heard the words of Christ but refused to listen until his Damascus road experience. Right now, are we going through our own Damascus road experience? Are we now ready to hear God's words and do His will?

This famine will get worse. Let us store up the word and be transformed by the renewal of our minds. Let us turn from a *church life* existence to a *Christ like* experience. Time is running out. Study the word and ask the Holy Spirit for understanding that we may be fortified to resist the enemy when he shall come in like a flood.

WEEKLY WEAPON: <u>I will strengthen myself in the Lord.</u>

1. ROMANS 8:35

   Who shall separate us from the love of Christ? shall tribulation, or distress, or persecution, or famine, or nakedness, or peril, or sword?

2. 1 TIMOTHY 6:19

   Laying up in store for themselves a good foundation against the time to come, that they may lay hold on eternal life.

3. ACTS 28:27

   For the heart of this people is waxed gross, and their ears are dull of hearing, and their eyes have they closed; lest they should see with their eyes, and hear with their ears, and understand with their heart, and should be converted, and I should heal them.

4. PROVERBS 28:9

   He that turneth away his ear from hearing the law, even his prayer shall be abomination.

5. 2 TIMOTHY 2:15

   Study to shew thyself approved unto God, a workman that needeth not to be ashamed, rightly dividing the word of truth.

6. PROVERBS 18:2

   A fool hath no delight in understanding, but that his heart may discover itself.

PREACH JESUS

"Then Philip opened his mouth, and began at the same scripture, and preached unto him Jesus."
Acts 8:35 KJV

The entire Bible is about Jesus, the Son of God. Like Phillip we are to study and gain understanding of the word so we can explain, with the aid of the Holy Spirit, the messages that are contained in the Bible to anyone who may need assistance.

We can start at any point of the Bible and tell the story of Jesus' life, mission and service. From the book of Genesis to the book of Revelation, the central theme is about Jesus, the Saviour of this world.

Both the Old and the New Testament provide information on the great cloud of witnesses that speak to us about salvation. In times like these when we face so many trials, we can find examples on how to cope by reading the word of God.

Let us not despair nor be depressed, God has already provided a way of escape for us. All we have to do is be obedient to His voice. Let us break the bread of life with someone today, just as Phillip did for the eunuch.

WEEKLY WEAPON: <u>I will search the scriptures for myself</u>

1. MATTHEW 26:56

But all this was done, that the scriptures of the prophets might be fulfilled. Then all the disciples forsook him, and fled.

2. LUKE 24:27

And beginning at Moses and all the prophets, he expounded unto them in all the scriptures the things concerning himself.

3. LUKE 24:45

Then opened he their understanding, that they might understand the scriptures,

4. JOHN 5:39

Search the scriptures; for in them ye think ye have eternal life: and they are they which testify of me.

5. 2 TIMOTHY 3:15

And that from a child thou hast known the holy scriptures, which are able to make thee wise unto salvation through faith which is in Christ Jesus.

6. ACTS 18:28

For he mightily convinced the Jews, and that publicly, shewing by the scriptures that Jesus was Christ.

STAY IN THE WORD

"Wherewithal shall a young man cleanse his way?
by taking heed thereto according to thy word."
Psalms 119:9 KJV

Christ performs miracles. The enemy produces magic. The transforming power of Christ is found in the word of God. Many of us who follow Christ will be deceived because we don't study the word for ourselves. We look for something miraculous to happen to transform our lives and the enemy knows this. Thus in his craft, he sprinkles a few magical potions around us and we are deceived.

The word of God is clear on how a man or woman will cleanse their way. It is by adhering to the word of God- obedience. The only way we can adhere is by diligent study and by faithful application of the word in our lives. The word says for us to be with Him, we must be without blemish or spot, yet we refuse to cleanse our ways - we think we will be transformed by some magic.

Study the word, love God, accept his spotless blood that was shed for us, and walk in faith living our lives in accordance with the word and having all our ways will be cleansed. This is the only way.

WEEKLY WEAPON: <u>God show me your way that I may follow</u>

<u>POWER TEXTS FOR THE WEEK</u>

1. <u>2 CORINTHIANS 11:14</u>

And no marvel; for Satan himself is transformed into an angel of light.

2. <u>2 THESSALONIANS 2:9</u>

Even him, whose coming is after the working of Satan with all power and signs and lying wonders,

3. <u>2 CORINTHIANS 2:11</u>

Lest Satan should get an advantage of us: for we are not ignorant of his devices.

4. <u>REVELATION 12:9</u>

And the great dragon was cast out, that old serpent, called the Devil, and Satan, which deceiveth the whole world: he was cast out into the earth, and his angels were cast out with him.

5. <u>2 SAMUEL 22:45</u>

Strangers shall submit themselves unto me: as soon as they hear, they shall be obedient unto me.

6. <u>TITUS 3:5</u>

Not by works of righteousness which we have done, but according to his mercy he saved us, by the washing of regeneration, and renewing of the Holy Ghost;

UNITY ONLY FOUND IN CHRIST

"Wherefore seeing we also are compassed about with so great a cloud of witnesses, let us lay aside every weight, and the sin which doth so easily beset us, and let us run with patience the race that is set before us, To the general assembly and church of the firstborn, which are written in heaven, and to God the Judge of all, and to the spirits of just men made perfect,"
Hebrews 12:1, 23 KJV

God will have ONE unified church. It will NOT be an interfaith church NOR will it be an ecumenical Church. The church of the Firstborn will comprise all whose names are written in the book of life in heaven. Those whose names are written there are the ones who have accepted Jesus's blood to make them justified and, thereby, are made perfect.

Those of us who will overcome sin must walk in the way of truth. The members of His church are the ones who follow the Lamb wherever He leads and are obedient to His examples and His way. Those who follow His every commandment will be His remnant church. To become a member of this congregation, we must study His word.

God will have the names of those who do as He (God) says entered into the book of life. It is NOT what your pastor/priest or pope or what is written in the church manual says; it is not what our family or friends say, it is not what our employer says. The only thing that matters in the end is our obedience to Christ. Let us commit our lives to God so we can become members of the Firstborn Church of heaven. We shall wear a crown of righteousness and shall be called by a new name. This will be our reward.

WEEKLY WEAPON: <u>I shall make my calling and election sure.</u>

<u>POWER TEXTS FOR THE WEEK</u>

1. <u>PSALMS 133:1</u>

Behold, how good and how pleasant it is for brethren to dwell together in unity!

2. <u>EPHESIANS 4:13</u>

Till we all come in the unity of the faith, and of the knowledge of the Son of God, unto a perfect man, unto the measure of the stature of the fulness of Christ:

3. <u>PROVERBS 16:5</u>

Every one that is proud in heart is an abomination to the LORD: though hand join in hand, he shall not be unpunished.

4. <u>EZRA 9:14</u>

Should we again break thy commandments, and join in affinity with the people of these abominations? wouldest not thou be angry with us till thou hadst consumed us, so that there should be no remnant nor escaping?

5. <u>1 CORINTHIANS 1:10</u>

Now I beseech you, brethren, by the name of our Lord Jesus Christ, that ye all speak the same thing, and that there be no divisions among you; but that ye be perfectly joined together in the same mind and in the same judgment.

6. <u>ZECHARIAH 2:11</u>

And many nations shall be joined to the LORD in that day, and shall be my people: and I will dwell in the midst of thee, and thou shalt know that the LORD of hosts hath sent me unto thee.

SPIRITUAL HARMONY

"Husbands, love your wives, even as Christ also
loved the church, and gave himself for it;"
Ephesians 5:25 KJV

There are many issues facing God's created beings in the world today. The abuse of loved ones is astounding. The principal reason can be found in the lack of persons abiding fully by the principles laid down in the word of God.

The situation of domestic abuse is rampant because gospel order is not being followed. Too many are romantically involved outside of the bands of holy matrimony or have been drawn together for purely selfish reasons.

Love is a principle that is holy, pure, and without contention, it is all forgiving & compassionate, preferring each other above self. It is not about emotions which are just about lust of the flesh and of the eye. Unholy acts cannot and should never be associated with the principle of love. Persons get involved in relationships that go nowhere, looking for love.

Christ says to us to experience His love, then pattern all other relationships after the true love principle found ONLY in Christ. Love, indeed, is the answer. Know Christ first, and then relationships will be entered into with the sole purpose of bringing glory to God. I shall start with me today, what about you?

WEEKLY WEAPON: <u>I will find harmony in the spirit of Christ</u>

<u>POWER TEXTS FOR THE WEEK</u>

1. <u>MATTHEW 24:12</u>

   And because iniquity shall abound, the love of many shall wax cold.

2. <u>ROMANS 13:10</u>

   Love worketh no ill to his neighbour: therefore love is the fulfilling of the law.

3. <u>2 JOHN 1:6</u>

   And this is love, that we walk after his commandments. This is the commandment, That, as ye have heard from the beginning, ye should walk in it.

4. <u>1 PETER 3:8</u>

   Finally, be ye all of one mind, having compassion one of another, love as brethren, be pitiful, be courteous:

5. <u>1 TIMOTHY 6:11</u>

   But thou, O man of God, flee these things; and follow after righteousness, godliness, faith, love, patience, meekness.

6. <u>Hebrews 4:3</u>

   Endeavouring to keep the unity of the Spirit in the bond of peace.

SEEKING A SIGN?

"But he answered and said unto them, An evil and adulterous generation seeketh after a sign; and there shall no sign be given to it, but the sign of the prophet Jonas:"
Matthew 12:39 KJV

There is a tendency for us to always lean on our own understanding and trust our senses, particularly sight and hearing, before we believe and are converted. Christ describes all such as evil and adulterous - we refuse to accept that God is a spirit and we must worship him in spirit. Our senses are of the flesh and these are always in conflict with the spirit. Belief, faith, and trust are all in the realms of the spirit, and it is upon these that we are called to serve God.

Jonah told the people of Nineveh to repent and without a sign they did just that. As we look around us and we see the events that the bible foretold are we now more inclined to give our lives fully over to Christ? When we get a sign we keep looking for more signs. Christ is calling us to walk by faith and not by sight; we are told this because in the last days Satan will use our senses to deceive us. If we are depending on signs to move in the right direction, we shall be forever lost. We will not be able to discern the signs of God from the deceptions of the enemy.

Looking for signs opens us up to being deceived, thus we are described as adulterous because we lack the faithfulness to abide in God, our Creator. The word of God is the spiritual food. Let us feed ourselves on the meat of the spirit.

WEEKLY WEAPON: <u>I trust the word of God above my sight.</u>

1. 2 CORINTHIANS 5:7
   (For we walk by faith, not by sight:)

2. 2 CORINTHIANS 10:3
   For though we walk in the flesh, we do not war after the flesh:

3. TITUS 3:3
   For we ourselves also were sometimes foolish, disobedient, deceived, serving divers lusts and pleasures, living in malice and envy, hateful, and hating one another.

4. HEBREWS 2:4
   God also bearing them witness, both with signs and wonders, and with divers miracles, and gifts of the Holy Ghost, according to his own will?

5. NUMBERS 14:11
   And the Lord said unto Moses, How long will this people provoke me? and how long will it be ere they believe me, for all the signs which I have shewed among them?

6. JEREMIAH 10:2
   Thus saith the LORD, Learn not the way of the heathen, and be not dismayed at the signs of heaven; for the heathen are dismayed at them.

EPHESUS

"Nevertheless I have somewhat against thee,
because thou hast left thy first love."
Revelation 2:4 KJV

As followers of Christ we are expected to overcome every short coming of the seven churches of Revelation. The first church, Ephesus, had lost its first love - Christ. Even as we sing and say 'Every day with Jesus is sweeter than the day before', do our lives really demonstrate that Christ is our first love? We speak against the evil around us, but yet we do not lift the banner of Christ as high as we ought.

We excuse sin as part of 'being human'. We accept the world's standard that none can be perfect, even though Christ says we must be perfect. We hold on to our own cherished idols which are in competition with Christ's requests that our first love should be seen in obedience to God. If we accept man's theory that none can be perfect, then we are saying to God that He could never be our first love. To accept such a theory, there will always be something or someone who will claim a higher place in our lives. We will seek to justify this as flaws of the being a human claiming the lie that Satan himself planted in our minds.

Christ tells us we are to overcome the flesh and live in the spirit. If Christ tells us that we can be overcomers then we can rest assured that He has equipped us with the capacity to do so. Let us give Christ our all. Let us ask forgiveness of God for having neglected our first love. Let us recommit and reconnect with our first love today and every day.

WEEKLY WEAPON: <u>God, I will make you my first love.</u>

1. <u>1 JOHN 4:4</u>

    Ye are of God, little children, and have overcome them: because greater is he that is in you, than he that is in the world.

2. <u>ROMANS 12:21</u>

    Be not overcome of evil, but overcome evil with good.

3. <u>REVELATION 17:14</u>

    These shall make war with the Lamb, and the Lamb shall overcome them: for he is Lord of lords, and King of kings: and they that are with him are called, and chosen, and faithful.

4. <u>ROMANS 3:4</u>

    God forbid: yea, let God be true, but every man a liar; as it is written, That thou mightest be justified in thy sayings, and mightest overcome when thou art judged.

5. <u>JOHN 16:33</u>

    These things I have spoken unto you, that in me ye might have peace. In the world ye shall have tribulation: but be of good cheer; I have overcome the world.

6. <u>1 JOHN 5:4</u>

    For whatsoever is born of God overcometh the world: and this is the victory that overcometh the world, even our faith.

SMYRNA

"I know thy works, and tribulation, and poverty,
(but thou art rich) and I know the blasphemy of them which
say they are Jews, and are not, but are the synagogue of
Satan."

Revelation 2:9 KJV

There are two sets of people who are involved in God's work today those who are genuine and those who are not. Amidst those who are earnestly trying to do God's will those who seek to please God in every way are many who profess to be followers, but are really Satan's seed. Even though those of Christ's household are in the minority, they follow Christ no matter how difficult the way seems. These understand their limitations and depend on God to overcome.

The other group is of a greater number and seem to hold sway at times giving the body of Christ a bad label. They look and behave like the world, their words and actions are not consistent with the will or words of God. Christ knows those that are of Satan's fold. Let us ask Christ to search our hearts today and remove any wicked ways within us that we may become vessels worthy of honour.

If we are not doing God's will and abiding by His laws, we are of Satan's synagogue, even though we may think we are of God's household. Let us not be fooled, God is not mocked; He knows the intent of every heart even when man's perceptions are different.

WEEKLY WEAPON: <u>Let me be true to you dear Lord</u>

1. <u>ISAIAH 4:1</u>

And in that day seven women shall take hold of one man, saying, We will eat our own bread, and wear our own apparel: only let us be called by thy name, to take away our reproach.

2. <u>GALATIONS 6:7</u>

Be not deceived; God is not mocked: for whatsoever a man soweth, that shall he also reap.

3. <u>MATTHEW 7:13</u>

Enter ye in at the strait gate: for wide is the gate, and broad is the way, that leadeth to destruction, and many there be which go in thereat:

4. <u>PSALMS 139:23</u>

Search me, O God, and know my heart: try me, and know my thoughts:

5. <u>OBADIAH 1:3</u>

The pride of thine heart hath deceived thee, thou that dwellest in the clefts of the rock, whose habitation is high; that saith in his heart, Who shall bring me down to the ground?

6. <u>EPHESIANS 6:6</u>

Not with eyeservice, as menpleasers; but as the servants of Christ, doing the will of God from the heart;

PERGAMOS

"So hast thou also them that hold the doctrine of the Nicolaitans, which thing I hate."
Revelation 2:15 KJV

God despises the heretical teaching of the Nicolaitans that men can do what they want and once they believe on God they will be saved. This doctrine promotes that the law of God is dead, and that grace, mercy and love have taken its place. It basically teaches that you can eat what you want, dress how you like, have as many partners as you fancy. Once self is happy and prosperous, this is evidence of Gods blessings. This belief would indeed make a mockery of most of the bible and the doctrine of Christ.

The word of God says this teaching is hated because it is not true. Today many who say they believe in God live lives in accordance with the doctrine of the Nicolaitans. This doctrine is what Satan is most comfortable with. Let God's people accept and believe in God, let them acknowledge His faithfulness, but let them live lives that give pleasure to self. Satan only requires persons to lay claim that they are imperfect, but they can strive to be perfect. Christ says His blood will make us perfect, so when we don't accept this offer, we are basically rejecting His gift. Christ teaches we must overcome every sin and make pleasing God our highest priority and everything else will be added.

Let us, therefore reject such teachings that promote self and other falsehoods, like the commandments are nailed to the cross and no longer binding. The Lord's Sabbath is still binding, just as the commandment not to steal or kill, etc. Let us put away the Nicolaitan doctrine and follow Christ's example.

WEEKLY WEAPON: <u>I will let go of Nicolatian teachings</u>

<u>POWER TEXTS FOR THE WEEK</u>

1. <u>PHILIPPIANS 4:13</u>

    I can do all things through Christ which strengtheneth me.

2. <u>ISAIAH 5:20</u>

    Woe unto them that call evil good, and good evil; that
    put darkness for light, and light for darkness; that put bitter for
    sweet, and sweet for bitter!

3. <u>JEREMIAH 44:23</u>

    Because ye have burned incense, and because ye have sinned
    against the LORD, and have not obeyed the voice of the LORD,
    nor walked in his law, nor in his statutes, nor in his
    testimonies; therefore this evil is happened unto you, as at this
    day.

4. <u>1 CORINTHIANS 15:56</u>

    The sting of death is sin; and the strength of sin is the law.

5. <u>MATTHEW 6:33</u>

    But seek ye first the kingdom of God, and his righteousness;
    and all these things shall be added unto you.

6. <u>2 PETER 2: 1-2</u>

    But there were **false** prophets also among the people, even as
    there shall be **false teachers** among you, who privily shall
    bring in damnable heresies, even denying the Lord that bought
    them, and bring upon themselves swift destruction. And many
    shall follow their pernicious ways; by reason of whom the way
    of truth shall be evil spoken of.

THYATIRA

"Notwithstanding I have a few things against thee, because thou sufferest that woman Jezebel, which calleth herself a prophetess, to teach and to seduce my servants to commit fornication, and to eat things sacrificed unto idols."
Revelation 2:20 KJV

This rebuke comes because we have allowed Jezebel like tendencies to enter the church. We have allowed man's traditions and customs to direct our worship, while ignoring the true doctrines of God.

Pagan practices have been adopted and brought before God's people by misguided church leaders, causing the people of God to err and offer strange gifts of worship to God. Like Elijah, who challenged the false prophets of Jezebel we are called upon to challenge any practice that is not according to the word of God. The church, represented as a woman in scripture, is used in Revelation to highlight that leaders and churches will arise and introduce false worship to God's people. However, God has given us a mind to reason, and choice for us to make our own decisions in following Him. He invites us to come and reason together so that our understanding will be guided by the Holy Spirit, and not by blind leaders.

We will not be led astray by false teachings if we diligently seek God's word. We are, therefore, called as individuals, to study the word of God and depend on the Holy Ghost to guide us into all truth. As we become knowledgeable about the things of God and notice false teachings we are called to challenge these and sound the alarm. We are the Elijahs just as John the Baptist was the Elijah in his day.

WEEKLY WEAPON: <u>I will not follow Jezebel's teachings</u>

1. **1 KINGS 21:25**

   But there was none like unto Ahab, which did sell himself to work wickedness in the sight of the LORD, whom Jezebel his wife stirred up.

2. **LUKE 6:39**

   And he spake a parable unto them, Can the blind lead the blind? shall they not both fall into the ditch?

3. **EPHESIANS 4:18**

   Having the understanding darkened, being alienated from the life of God through the ignorance that is in them, because of the blindness of their heart:

4. **JEREMIAH 5:31**

   The prophets prophesy falsely, and the priests bear rule by their means; and my people love to have it so: and what will ye do in the end thereof?

5. **1 TIMOTHY 4:16**

   Take heed unto thyself, and unto the doctrine; continue in them: for in doing this thou shalt both save thyself, and them that hear thee.

6. **1 TIMOTHY 4:1**

   Now the Spirit speaketh expressly, that in the latter times some shall depart from the faith, giving heed to seducing spirits, and doctrines of devils;

SARDIS

"Be watchful, and strengthen the things which remain, that are ready to die: for I have not found thy works perfect before God."
Revelation 3:2 KJV

The message to this church is to be watchful and strengthen those things which are about to die. This charge is part of the great commission. We are to speak the name of Christ in season and out of season to men everywhere. We are to ensure that sin is called by its right name every time and never allow evil to be called good or good to be called evil.

We are called to be watchmen upon Zion's walls, to be ready to give the trumpet a distinct sound. Thus, we have to be in tune with the word of God, understanding prophecy and loving one another, working for the Master and never becoming distracted, but being obedient to the end. We must accept the call to live in perfection, no matter what the world says.

How do we strengthen those things that remain that are about to die? Firstly, we have to know what is remaining. Is it morals standards, is it health practices, is it the law of God, and/or is it biblical doctrines? To know what is remaining, we have to study the past and examine the present, and based on that comparison, we would then know where to add our voices and apply our strength to those things.

To him that watches, Christ shall not appear as a thief in the night, for he/she shall be ready with lamps trimmed and burning to receive the soon coming Lord. Be ye watchful.

WEEKLY WEAPON: <u>I will not die outside of Christ</u>

<u>POWER TEXTS FOR THE WEEK</u>

1. <u>EZEKIEL 33:6</u>

But if the watchman see the sword come, and blow not the trumpet, and the people be not warned; if the sword come, and take any person from among them, he is taken away in his iniquity; but his blood will I require at the watchman's hand.

2. <u>ISAIAH 62:6</u>

I have set watchmen upon thy walls, O Jerusalem, which shall never hold their peace day nor night: ye that make mention of the LORD, keep not silence,

3. <u>1 PETER 4:7</u>

But the end of all things is at hand: be ye therefore sober, and watch unto prayer.

4. <u>2 TIMOTHY 4:5</u>

But watch thou in all things, endure afflictions, do the work of an evangelist, make full proof of thy ministry.

5. <u>1 THESSALONIANS 5:6</u>

Therefore let us not sleep, as do others; but let us watch and be sober.

6. <u>HABAKKUK 2:1</u>

I will stand upon my watch, and set me upon the tower, and will watch to see what he will say unto me, and what I shall answer when I am reproved.

PHILADELPHIA

"Him that overcometh will I make a pillar in the temple of my God, and he shall go no more out: and I will write upon him the name of my God, and the name of the city of my God, which is new Jerusalem, which cometh down out of heaven from my God: and I will write upon him my new name."

Revelation 3:12 KJV

There is a new name awaiting all those over comers. This is Christ's seal of approval for a life that has not denied His name and has kept His word. To such a person is the door opened, and they will be kept by God in the hour of temptation which the entire world will face.

Each one of us is making a choice daily: to hold fast to the word of God and enter the open door or to go with man's traditions and his words and stay out of God's kingdom. The choice is ours. Either we reject the pleasures of the world and walk with Christ or cling to the allure of the world and reject Christ. Choose today whom you will serve. We say we love God and each other but our actions and motives show what our true affections and affiliations are. Being a pillar in the house of the Lord requires integrity and strength. As a pillar, we have to be ready to stand up like other biblical and modern pillars we know about. To be prepared to stand like those pillars, we must be strong in the Lord. Let us not waver in doing justice, mercy, humility and righteousness.

The door is still open for anyone who desires to be a pillar in the house of God. However, His offer is limited in time; it will not remain open forever. Choose Christ today.

WEEKLY WEAPON: <u>Lord, make me a pillar in Your house.</u>

<u>POWER TEXTS FOR THE WEEK</u>

1. <u>GALATIANS 2:9</u>

And when James, Cephas, and John, who seemed to be pillars, perceived the grace that was given unto me, they gave to me and Barnabas the right hands of fellowship; that we should go unto the heathen, and they unto the circumcision.

2. <u>COLOSSIANS 1:11</u>

Strengthened with all might, according to his glorious power, unto all patience and longsuffering with joyfulness;

3. <u>PSALMS 18:32</u>

It is God that girdeth me with strength, and maketh my way perfect.

4. <u>PROVERBS 24:14</u>

If thou faint in the day of adversity, thy strength is small.

5. <u>GALATIANS 6:10</u>

As we have therefore opportunity, let us do good unto all men, especially unto them who are of the household of faith.

6. <u>HEBREWS 8:10</u>

For this is the covenant that I will make
with the house of Israel after those days, saith the Lord; I will put my laws into their mind, and write them in their hearts: and I will be to them a God, and they shall be to me a people:

LAODICEA

"Because thou sayest, I am rich, and increased with goods, and have need of nothing; and knowest not that thou art wretched, and miserable, and poor, and blind, and naked:"

Revelation 3:17 KJV

This is the message to the last of the seven churches - us church goers and people living in the 21st century, or in the final days of earth's history. It is a rebuke to us who claim to have wisdom but are ignorant of spiritual matters and refuse to understand that we are under Satan's deception. We don't recognize that we are wretched; because we fake happiness, allowing pride to keep us from total surrender to God. This group is very similar to the inhabitants of Sodom before fire rained down on them. They were seeking pleasure, not realising that this was merely showcasing their state of wretchedness. Our misery is seen even as we seek more and more events and things to keep ourselves entertained.

We are poor because we lack understanding of what it costs to have eternal life. We are blind, for we see all the signs, yet we can't make the connections that exist between our state, and that of the world. Christ calls to us to be separate from a sin sick world by examining our own actions and standards and those of the world. Finally, we are naked, for we fail to fully put on Christ's righteousness. We look at ourselves and feel we are clothed in righteousness because of our actions that seem good to us. We go to church every week, we pray every day, we can recite scriptures, we may even fast from time to time, but in spite of all this, we would not overcome all sin and this exposes us to a holy God, thus we are naked. The offer today is to get real and get ready.

WEEKLY WEAPON: <u>I will not be deceived any longer.</u>

<u>POWER TEXTS FOR THE WEEK</u>

1. <u>1 JOHN 3:7</u>

   Little children, let no man deceive you: he that doeth righteousness is righteous, even as he is righteous.

2. <u>ROMANS 7:24</u>

   O wretched man that I am! who shall deliver me from the body of this death?

3. <u>JAMES 5:1</u>

   Go to now, ye rich men, weep and howl for your miseries that shall come upon you.

4. <u>AMOS 4:11</u>

   I have overthrown some of you, as God overthrew Sodom and Gomorrah, and ye were as a firebrand plucked out of the burning: yet have ye not returned unto me, saith the LORD.

5. <u>PROVERBS 4:19</u>

   The way of the wicked is as darkness: they know not at what they stumble.

6. <u>ISAIAH 66:4</u>

   I also will choose their delusions, and will bring their fears upon them; because when I called, none did answer; when I spake, they did not hear: but they did evil before mine eyes, and chose that in which I delighted not.

GOD'S DECLARATION
"I Jesus have sent mine angel to testify unto you
these things in the churches. I am the root and the offspring
of David, and the bright and morning star."
Revelation 22:16 KJV

Christ has sent His angel and His prophets to us to get us ready for the time of the end. Just as it was in the days of Noah and in the days of Lot, when judgement rained down by a flood and by fire respectively, the majority of God's people had not heeded the warnings and were not ready for the Day of Judgment. We are living in a time when, again, most of God's people are not ready for his judgment.

In Noah's day, the people heard the message and scoffed. In Lot's day, there was open rebellion against the word and men did as they pleased. God had Noah prepare food and an ark. He took Lot out of the city into the mountain and provided for him.

The examples are for us to follow. God's church has been warned and must be ready. I am supposed to be the church and so are you, but are we really? The church is told to spread the three angels' messages before the seven last plagues come upon the earth. These plagues will impact the world's health, economy, spirituality, climate, morality, politics, and culture. We have been warned in God's word but are we listening? If we are listening, what are we doing about the call?

Let us commit to being obedient so that the plagues will not fall upon us. God's people will be sealed and will escape those plagues. First, we must understand the three angels' messages and tell the world about Christ's soon return.

WEEKLY WEAPON: <u>I will proclaim God's declaration</u>

1. <u>2 PETER 2:6</u>

   And turning the cities of Sodom and Gomorrha into ashes condemned them with an overthrow, making them an ensample unto those that after should live ungodly;

2. <u>Revelations 14: 6-7</u>

   And I saw another angel fly in the midst of heaven, having the everlasting gospel to preach unto them that dwell on the earth, and to every nation, and kindred, and tongue, and people,... Fear God, and give glory to him; for the hour of his judgment is come: …

3. <u>Revelation 14: 8</u>

   And there followed another angel, saying, Babylon is fallen, is fallen, that great city, because she made all nations drink of the wine of the wrath of her fornication.

4. <u>Revelation 14:9</u>

   And the third angel followed them, saying with a loud voice, If any man worship the beast and his image, and receive his mark in his forehead, or in his hand,

5. <u>Revelation 15:1</u>

   And I saw another sign in heaven, great and marvellous, seven angels having the seven last plagues; for in them is filled up the wrath of God.

6. <u>Matthew 24:37</u>

   But as the days of Noah were, so shall also the coming of the Son of man be.

SCRIPTURES FORETELL

"And beginning at Moses and all the prophets, he expounded unto them in all the scriptures the things concerning himself."

Luke 24:27 KJV

We do not now fully understand the nature of the great conflict and why the calamities of the world are coming to us on every side. Real understanding can only come from the scriptures and from having an experience of knowing Christ for ourselves.

Christ used the scriptures to explain the events and times to the two disciples going to Emmaus. They finally understood all its meaning only after they had sat down together for a meal and He broke bread with them. Very often, we have heard or read the scriptures but it will only make sense when we decide to have fellowship with Christ.

Let us sit down and invite the Holy Spirit to fellowship and teach us the scriptures. As we spend time with Christ, we shall understand why the world is in the state it is in today and why we have to walk away from the things of the world and be hid in Christ. In real terms, if you have a friend and they know very little about you, would you call that person a friend or an acquaintance? Christ wants to be our friend, so we have to know everything about him.

Let's pray, study and fellowship with the Holy Spirit and learn about our Friend. We must know what He has gone through and where He is now: we must have a clear understanding of when he is coming again. Let's be friends of Jesus now.

WEEKLY WEAPON: <u>I must KNOW who Jesus is.</u>

1. **EPHESIANS 6:12**

   For we wrestle not against flesh and blood, but against principalities, against powers, against the rulers of the darkness of this world, against spiritual wickedness in high places.

2. **2 CORINTHIANS 13:2**

   I told you before, and foretell you, as if I were present, the second time; and being absent now I write to them which heretofore have sinned, and to all other, that, if I come again, I will not spare:

3. **MARK 13:23**

   But take ye heed: behold, I have foretold you all things.

4. **ACTS 3:24**

   Yea, and all the prophets from Samuel and those that follow after, as many as have spoken, have likewise foretold of these days.

5. **1 JOHN 2:27**

   But the anointing which ye have received of him abideth in you, and ye need not that any man teach you: but as the same anointing teacheth you of all things, and is truth, and is no lie, and even as it hath taught you, ye shall abide in him.

6. **HEBREWS 8:14**

   And they shall not teach every man his neighbour, and every man his brother, saying, Know the Lord: for all shall know me, from the least to the greatest.

IN HIS PRESENCE

"If, when evil cometh upon us, as the sword, judgment, or pestilence, or famine, we stand before this house, and in thy presence, (for thy name is in this house,) and cry unto thee in our affliction, then thou wilt hear and help."

2 Chronicles 20:9 KJV

God's grace and mercy is without measure. He can turn back any calamity that may face His people. God's people can claim every promise in His word, but the overriding question is, Are we His people?

The Bible says God's people are characterized as those who are obedient to His word, keep His commandments and have the faith of Jesus. How do we measure up today? His door is open today and He says to us harden not your hearts. He says if my people who are called by my name will be humble, pray, seek His face and turn from evil then He will hear, forgive and heal.

This is the promise of God. Don't let us pass up the opportunity to be called by His name and stand in His presence. It is time to examine our character against God's standard, His living testimony, the Bible.

WEEKLY WEAPON: <u>I will stay in thy presence O Lord.</u>

1. **JUDE 1:24**

   Now unto him that is able to keep you from falling, and to present you faultless before the presence of his glory with exceeding joy,

2. **PSALMS 16:11**

   Thou wilt shew me the path of life: in thy presence is fulness of joy; at thy right hand there are pleasures for evermore.

3. **ZEPHANIAH 1:7**

   Hold thy peace at the presence of the Lord GOD: for the day of the LORD is at hand: for the LORD hath prepared a sacrifice, he hath bid his guests.

4. **PSALMS 13:20**

   Thou shalt hide them in the secret of thy presence from the pride of man: thou shalt keep them secretly in a pavilion from the strife of tongues.

5. **JEREMIAH 23:22**

   But if they had stood in my counsel, and had caused my people to hear my words, then they should have turned them from their evil way, and from the evil of their doings.

6. **PSALMS 78:1**

   Give ear, O my people, to my law: incline your ears to the words of my mouth.

SUN WORSHIP

"And he brought me into the inner court of the Lord's house, and, behold, at the door of the temple of the Lord, between the porch and the altar, were about five and twenty men, with their backs toward the temple of the Lord, and their faces toward the east; and they worshipped the sun toward the east."

Ezekiel 8:16 KJV

In the vision that was shown to Ezekiel, this abomination was the last in a line of abominations shown to Ezekiel. Notice, this vision is in the church with the church goers, who have turned against the Lord in His holy temple and submit to sun worship. Many church goers feel that they must be worshipping God because they are attending church, not realising that worship is more than church attendance, it is our life's dedication.

This will become clearer as mandated Sunday worship is imminent. Many do not realise the importance of Sunday worship. It has a history and destination that is integrally tied to the mark of the beast. Persons who accept Sunday as the Lord's Day have been misguided by blind leaders, not realising it is actually sun worship. The word of God is clear on this matter and is easily understood if we put Christ first and determine to follow in His way.

In the final crisis people will be led by church leaders pushing for a day to rest, thinking that this will please God and help return morality to this world. We see this movement gaining momentum in the US, with the evangelical leaders pushing the president on religious matters, bringing church and state into an unholy alliance. Such an act will be justified as a solution to climate issues, but, in effect it is the last step of apostasy, since it goes against God's 4th commandment.

WEEKLY WEAPON: <u>I will follow Jesus.</u>

<u>POWER TEXTS FOR THE WEEK</u>

1. <u>DEUTERONOMY 4:19</u>

   And lest thou lift up thine eyes unto heaven, and when thou seest the sun, and the moon, and the stars, even all the host of heaven, shouldest be driven to worship them, and serve them, which the LORD thy God hath divided unto all nations under the whole heaven.

2. <u>JEREMIAH 8:2</u>

   And they shall spread them before the sun, and the moon, and all the host of heaven, whom they have loved, and whom they have served, and after whom they have walked, and whom they have sought, and whom they have worshipped: …

3. <u>HEBREWS 4:8</u>

   For if Jesus had given them rest, then would he not afterward have spoken of another day.

4. <u>ISAIAH 33:6</u>

   And wisdom and knowledge shall be the stability of thy times, and strength of salvation: the fear of the Lord is his treasure.

5. <u>GENESIS 2:3</u>

   And God blessed the seventh day, and sanctified it: because that in it he had rested from all his work which God created and made.

6. <u>LEVITICUS 10:10</u>

   And that ye may put difference between holy and unholy, and between unclean and clean;

WAY OF ESCAPE

"Watch ye therefore, and pray always, that ye may be accounted worthy to escape all these things that shall come to pass, and to stand before the Son of man."
Luke 21:36 KJV

Jesus explained to His disciples all the various signs that would come to pass in the last days (pestilence, heavenly wonders, earthquakes, food shortages etc. all in different places) and he tells us how to escape it. He tells us to move out of the cities and not to become involved in the cares of this life.

He says watch (look for the signs and link it to the times) and pray without ceasing. This is what we must do to keep our minds stayed on Christ and as a way of escape. We are not to be distracted by the issues that will arise and seek to draw us into pointless conflicts that take our minds away from being made ready for our Lord's soon return.

If we understand the signs of the time what manner of people are we supposed to be? We should be wise, without being pompous, gentle, but being bold for the truth, empathetic but speaking truth in love, lift high the standard for Christ but without starting a rebellion. Seek to model Christ, speak when warranted but show kindness at all times to everyone. Recognise that the loss of one soul brings tremendous pain to our Lord.

WEEKLY WEAPON: <u>Lord, I will escape as you lead me</u>

1. <u>2 TIMOTHY 3:1</u>
    This know also, that in the last days perilous times shall come.

2. <u>2 PETER 3:3</u>
    Knowing this first, that there shall come in
    the last days scoffers, walking after their own lusts,

3. <u>MICAH 4:1</u>
    But in the last days it shall come to pass, that the mountain of
    the house of the LORD shall be established in the top of the
    mountains, and it shall be exalted above the hills; and people
    shall flow unto it.

4. <u>ISAIAH 62:11</u>
    Behold, the LORD hath proclaimed unto the end of the world,
    Say ye to the daughter of Zion, Behold, thy salvation cometh;
    behold, his reward is with him, and his work before him.

5. <u>HEBREWS 9:6</u>
    For then must he often have suffered
    since the foundation of the world: but now once
    in the end of the world hath he appeared to put away sin
    by the sacrifice of himself.

6. <u>1 Corinthians 10:11</u>
    Now all these things happened unto them for examples:
    and they are written for our admonition, upon
    whom the ends of the world are come.

PLEASING GOD

"When a man's ways please the Lord, he maketh even his enemies to be at peace with him."
Proverbs 16:7 KJV

There is a choice to be made by each one of us. We must decide whether we prefer the praise of God or the praise of man. "For do I now persuade men, or God? or do I seek to please men? for if I yet pleased men, I should not be the servant of Christ." Galatians 1:10.

We are pleasing man when we go in opposition to God's will and his way. Keeping God's commandments indicate we are seeking to please God for this is His will and His way.

Disobeying any part of His law means we have chosen to please man instead of God. In choosing man and/or self over God, we are choosing the devil, for there are only two camps into which we can fall: the camp of God or the camp of Satan. So are you pleasing the Lord? Know that your biggest enemy is Satan and while he (Satan) will seek to deceive many with overtures of calls for peace and goodwill do not give place to him. Seek only to please God.

Remember, not everyone who cries out that they believe in God are giving Him pleasure. God wants all of us. That is the only time He will have pleasure in us.

Choose you this day whom you will serve, for the choice we make today will determine where we will spend our eternity. **WEEKLY WEAPON**: <u>I choose to give God pleasure.</u>

<u>POWER TEXTS FOR THE WEEK</u>

1. <u>2 TIMOTHY 2:4</u>

No man that warreth entangleth himself with the affairs of this life; that he may please him who hath chosen him to be a soldier.

2. <u>EPHESIANS 1:4</u>

According as he hath chosen us in him before the foundation of the world, that we should be holy and without blame before him in love:

3. <u>MARK 13:20</u>

And except that the Lord had shortened those days, no flesh should be saved: but for the elect's sake, whom he hath **chose**n, he hath shortened the days.

4. <u>MATTHEW 22:14</u>

For many are called, but few are chosen.

5. <u>PSALMS 105:43</u>

And he brought forth his people with joy, and his chosen with gladness:

6. <u>ISAIAH 41:9</u>

Thou whom I have taken from the ends of the earth, and called thee from the chief men thereof, and said unto thee, Thou art my servant; I have **chose**n thee, and not cast thee away.

BAPTIZED IN THE SPIRIT

"But the fruit of the Spirit is love, joy, peace, longsuffering, gentleness, goodness, faith, Meekness, temperance: against such there is no law."
Galatians 5:22-23 KJV

When the Holy Ghost is come upon us, it will be evidenced by the fruit of the Spirit. Every follower of Christ should be seeking to attain the baptism of the Holy Spirit without such a baptism; we will not receive the fruit which is needed for us to be like Christ. The goal of every follower of Christ is to be like Christ, thus we will be severely tested and tempted as He was.

To overcome the world, we must cease to walk in the flesh but rather in the spirit. We must seek the baptism of the Spirit that we may walk as a new person in the Spirit. The fruit of the Spirit displays we are over-comers of sin and worthy of receiving the crown of righteousness. Many, who are baptized and placed their names on the record of a local church, use this changed status as their trophy of salvation. Men are often satisfied with this trophy alone but is this it enough for God? Christ wants to see a total surrender and that is done where no man can see – in the heart.

When such a conversion occurs the individual and those around will see the fruit of this life – love, joy, longsuffering, gentleness, goodness, faith, meekness, and temperance must be seen. Have we seen this fruit in our lives? If you have not, then that conversion process is not yet complete, that is why we have to stay in Christ and allow this process to be completed and we must pray for others to receive this baptism of the Spirit and of fire also. Let us examine ourselves and be ready to fight the good fight of faith, for faith is the victory that overcomes the word.

WEEKLY WEAPON: <u>Baptise me in the Spirit, Lord</u>.

1. **MARK 1:8**

   I indeed have baptized you with water: but he shall baptize
   you with the Holy Ghost.

2. **LUKE 3:16**

   John answered, saying unto them all, I indeed baptize you with
   water; but one mightier than I cometh, the latchet of whose
   shoes I am not worthy to unloose: he shall baptize you with
   the Holy Ghost and with fire:

3. **GALATIANS 3:27**

   For as many of you as have been baptized into Christ have put
   on Christ.

4. **EPHESIANS 5:9**

   (For the fruit of the Spirit is in all goodness and righteousness
   and truth;)

5. **REVELATION 4:11**

   Thou art worthy, O Lord, to receive glory and honour and
   power: for thou hast created all things, and for
   thy pleasure they are and were created.

6. **2 THESSALONIANS 1:11**

   Wherefore also we pray always for you, that our God would
   count you worthy of this calling, and fulfil all the
   good pleasure of his goodness, and the work of faith with
   power:

DEARLY BELOVED

"Having therefore these promises, dearly beloved, let us cleanse ourselves from all filthiness of the flesh and spirit, perfecting holiness in the fear of God."
2 Corinthians 7:1 KJV

Sitting before us are two options:
1. The promise of an everlasting life with Christ
2. The reward of eternal damnation.
Why do we treat this matter of our destiny so lightly? We hunger and thirst after the fleeting pleasures of this world instead of after righteousness, refusing to invest in life everlasting. While we say we want life everlasting, we live our lives in opposition to what is necessary for obtaining such. We are called to cleanse ourselves from worldly influences and live lives that treasure holiness, fearing God, always. We must consider such things like what would God have us eat, where He would have us live, how and when He want us to have worship Him, how we should be living and preparing to meet Him. All these things should be preoccupations that keep our attention focused on Christ and we will find these answers in His word.

We must follow ALL of Christ's examples and His words to obtain the precious promise. Let us commit today to walk the narrow path no matter what men say. Christ will not accept a 99% investment. It must be 100 %. Satan on the other hand will gladly accept 1%, knowing that if he gets that 1%, you can't give Christ your all. Choose wisely, choose life choose Christ.

WEEKLY WEAPON: <u>I will accept the cleansing of God</u>

1. PROVERBS 30:12

There is a generation that are pure in their own eyes, and yet is not washed from their filthiness.

2. EPHESIANS 5:4

Neither filthiness, nor foolish talking, nor jesting, which are not convenient: but rather giving of thanks.

3. JAMES 1:21

Wherefore lay apart all filthiness and superfluity of naughtiness, and receive with meekness the engrafted word, which is able to save your souls.

4. PHILIPPIANS 3:12

Not as though I had already attained, either were already perfect: but I follow after, if that I may apprehend that for which also I am apprehended of Christ Jesus.

5. ROMANS 9:25

As he saith also in Osee, I will call them my people, which were not my people; and her beloved, which was not beloved.

6. COLOSSIANS 4:12

Epaphras, who is one of you, a servant of Christ, saluteth you, always labouring fervently for you in prayers, that ye may stand perfect and complete in all the will of God.

DAILY CONFLICT

"For we wrestle not against flesh and blood, but against principalities, against powers, against the rulers of the darkness of this world, against spiritual wickedness in high places."

Ephesians 6:12 KJV

The enemy of God is continuously plotting 24/7 how to cause mankind to sin and to be separated from its Saviour. The evil one will use anyone and anything at his disposal to aid in his plan of distraction from the truth. Those who pledge to follow Christ are his primary target. We should not be misguided into believing that those for whom we care would do things that will cause us to harbour anger, resentment and distrust. Behind these actions is a more sinister conflict at play.

The enemy will have us think it is a person who is responsible for some of our unhappiness, when it is Satan, himself, behind every evil in our homes, our schools, the work place, the government, on the street and/or especially in the church. We have to ask God for discernment and the presence of mind to recognize the conflicts we have is because of the devil and sin no matter how it is manifested. The only way to overcome the enemy is to stay firmly on the side of Christ, staying in the word and out of the world.

Christ's example to us is the effective use of the sword, which is the word of God. Today, get armed and stay ready. The conflict is real. The enemy is attacking on every side. However, God is able to keep us, if we cover ourselves with His love.

WEEKLY WEAPON: <u>I will stay under the cover of Christ.</u>

1. <u>MATTHEW 10:36</u>

   And a man's foes shall be they of his own household.

2. <u>EPHESIANS 2:19</u>

   Now therefore ye are no more strangers and foreigners, but fellowcitizens with the saints, and of the household of God;

3. <u>PROVERBS 15:1</u>

   A soft answer turneth away wrath: but grievous words stir up anger.

4. <u>EXODUS 15:9</u>

   The enemy said, I will pursue, I will overtake, I will divide the spoil; my lust shall be satisfied upon them; I will draw my sword, my hand shall destroy them.

5. <u>JAMES 4:4</u>

   Ye adulterers and adulteresses, know ye not that the friendship of the world is enmity with God? whosoever therefore will be a friend of the world is the enemy of God.

6. <u>LUKE 10:19</u>

   Behold, I give unto you power to tread on serpents and scorpions, and over all the power of the enemy: and nothing shall by any means hurt you.

SECOND DEATH

"He that hath an ear, let him hear what the Spirit saith unto the churches; He that overcometh shall not be hurt of the second death."
Revelation 2:11 KJV

Most persons are scared to death of death, for we dread the thought of not seeing family and friends ever again. The word of God teaches us that what we *should* worry about is the second death. He that overcomes will not taste of that second death. We need to overcome sin in order not to be hurt in the second death.

The first death is a sleep that we shall awake from either at Christ second advent or His third advent. If we overcome sin now and fall asleep (die), then we will be raised at Christ's second coming and will not be hurt by the second death. Let us pray and work to overcome sin now to avoid being hurt in the second death, for this is the true purpose of our life now.

If we die in Christ, we will not see the second death. It will be the same for our loved ones if they, too, die in Christ. Our preoccupation and main goal should be that we and our family live in such a way that adheres to God's laws and be obedient to His every word. This will ensure that our names are written in the book of life. Let us preach this message of salvation to one another, strengthening each other's resolve to stay focused on Christ. Let us live in such a way that we do not fear this first death but let us dread of the second death.

WEEKLY WEAPON: <u>I will live now to avoid the second death</u>

1. REVELATIONS 20:14

    And death and hell were cast into the lake of fire. This is
    the second death.

2. REVELATIONS 20:6

    Blessed and holy is he that hath part in the first resurrection:
    on such the second death hath no power, but they shall be
    priests of God and of Christ, and shall reign with him a
    thousand years.

3. REVELATIONS 20:5

    But the rest of the dead lived not again until the thousand
    years were finished. This is the first resurrection.

4. REVELATIONS 21: 8

    But the fearful, and unbelieving, and the abominable, and
    murderers, and whoremongers, and sorcerers, and idolaters,
    and all liars, shall have their part in the lake which burneth
    with fire and brimstone: which is the second death.

5. ROMANS 6:16

    Know ye not, that to whom ye yield yourselves servants to
    obey, his servants ye are to whom ye obey; whether of sin
    unto death, or of obedience unto righteousness?

6. ROMANS 6: 23

    For the wages of sin is death; but the gift of God is eternal life
    through Jesus Christ our Lord.

NOT EVEN THE APPEARANCE

"Abstain from all appearance of evil."
1 Thessalonians 5:22 KJV

There must be a clear distinction between the children of light or of the day, and those children of the darkness or of the night. There ought to be no misunderstanding about the difference between one and the other. This difference must be driven from a deep conviction that can only be felt if the Holy Ghost is residing within. Every child of light must abstain from every appearance of evil.

If any type of behaviour, speech, dress, association etc. can be interpreted as evil, the child of the day should never be associated with any such activity or scene. The child of light must be peaceful, law abiding and obedient to the word of God; sober, ever vigilant, warning and exhorting fellow brethren of the soon return of our Lord and King. Today, as we seek to abstain from ALL appearances of evil, let us examine every thought, word and deed, and pray for the Holy Spirit to consume and guide us.

As we come into the homestretch, we have got to put on blinders and let not one drop of evil tarnish or mar our characters. Why would we let fashion keep us from eternity? Why would we allow a sexual relationship to keep us away for Christ? Why would we allow silly music, intoxicating drinks, and indulgence of forbidden foods, idle chatter, vain traditions and the like? Let no evil thought enter in and cause us to stumble.

WEEKLY WEAPON: <u>All for Christ! I shall surrender.</u>

<u>POWER TEXTS FOR THE WEEK</u>

1. <u>EZEKIEL 14:20</u>

Though Noah, Daniel, and Job were in it, as I live, saith the Lord GOD, they shall deliver neither son nor daughter; they shall but deliver their own souls by their righteousness.

2. <u>TITUS 2:8</u>

Sound speech, that cannot be condemned; that he that is of the contrary part may be ashamed, having no evil thing to say of you.

3. <u>1 PETER 5:8</u>

Be sober, be vigilant; because your adversary the devil, as a roaring lion, walketh about, seeking whom he may devour:

4. <u>ROMANS 1:18</u>

For the wrath of God is revealed from heaven against all ungodliness and unrighteousness of men, who hold the truth in unrighteousness;

5. <u>2 CORINTHIANS 6:17</u>

Wherefore come out from among them, and be ye separate, saith the Lord, and touch not the unclean thing; and I will receive you.

6. <u>EPHESIANS 5:5</u>

For this ye know, that no whoremonger, nor unclean person, nor covetous man, who is an idolater, hath any inheritance in the kingdom of Christ and of God.

STRANGE FIRE

"And Nadab and Abihu, the sons of Aaron, took either of them his censer, and put fire therein, and put incense thereon, and offered strange fire before the Lord, which he commanded them not. And there went out fire from the Lord, and devoured them, and they died before the Lord."

Leviticus 10:1-2 KJV

After lengthy explanations and demonstrations of the power of God, the sons of Aaron offered God strange fire and were destroyed for it. Cain slew his brother, Abel because his sacrifice to God was refused. Uzzah stretched forth his hand to steady the Ark of the Covenant and was struck dead. These are just a few cases of persons who knew what the Lord requested but chose to do differently. This was all strange fire before God.

What strange fire are we offering the Lord today? Is it something that He never requested? Don't let us miss out on life everlasting by giving God what He never commanded. Let us be obedient to his commands. He tells us how and when we are to worship Him. His word says clearly what He will accept and what He will not. Let us not do our own thing and say it is our worship to Him. All that would be is 'strange fire' for which we will be destroyed. Obedience is the best sacrifice. The day of worship is a key part of worship that God has requested and many feel it is no longer important. He required His seventh day Sabbath to be kept holy. Any other day we seek to give to God is like bringing strange fire before Him. He tells us in His word what happens after death yet we tell persons that their dead loved ones are in heaven. This too is strange fire. While there is time let us consider what fire we present to God.

WEEKLY WEAPON: <u>I will not offer any strange fire to God</u>.

1. **MALACHI 2:11**

   Judah hath dealt treacherously, and an abomination is committed in Israel and in Jerusalem; for Judah hath profaned the holiness of the LORD which he loved, and hath married the daughter of a strange god.

2. **EXODUS 30:9**

   Ye shall offer no strange incense thereon, nor burnt sacrifice, nor meat offering; neither shall ye pour drink offering thereon.

3. **ISAIAH 17:10**

   Because thou hast forgotten the God of thy salvation, and hast not been mindful of the rock of thy strength, therefore shalt thou plant pleasant plants, and shalt set it with strange slips:

4. **JUDE 1:7**

   Even as Sodom and Gomorrha, and the cities about them in like manner, giving themselves over to fornication, and going after strange flesh, are set forth for an example, suffering the vengeance of eternal fire.

5. **HEBREWS 13:9**

   Be not carried about with divers and strange doctrines. For it is a good thing that the heart be established with grace; not with meats, which have not profited them that have been occupied therein.

6. **PSALMS 81:9**

   There shall no strange god be in thee; neither shalt thou worship any strange god.

PAGANISM

"Thus saith the Lord, Learn not the way of the heathen, and be not dismayed at the signs of heaven; for the heathen are dismayed at them."

Jeremiah 10:2 KJV

Paganism is a system of worship and an acceptance of teachings and belief in multiple gods of the universe. A heathen in this context operates outside of God's expressed words and can be described as a pagan or a non-believer in God. While paganism is not mentioned in the Bible, the word heathen is mentioned. We are cautioned as God's people not to learn the way of the heathen, which leads to accepting customs and traditions of false worship (paganism).

The heathen see the signs of heaven also and are dismayed. God's people must show a different way that lights a path to Christ, away from every false god and false teachings. If the teaching is not found in the bible it is possibly best to not embrace. There are several major traditions that are pagan in origin. Christmas, Easter, Lent, Valentine's day, Mother's day, Father's day to name a few of the popular celebrations that all have origins in paganism. Practices like prayer circles and hand holding in prayers no relation to the Bible but have been embraced by most churches. Remember, we are not to learn the way of the heathen.

Let us commit to follow only the word and will of Christ and be not distracted by the vain practices/traditions of the heathen and pagan.

WEEKLY WEAPON: <u>'Solo Scriptura' I shall abide by scripture</u>

1. <u>PSALMS 2:1</u>

Why do the heathen rage, and the people imagine a vain thing?

2. <u>ZEPHANIAH 2:11</u>

The LORD will be terrible unto them: for he will famish all the gods of the earth; and men shall worship him, every one from his place, even all the isles of the heathen.

3. <u>MALACHI 1:14</u>

But cursed be the deceiver, which hath in his flock a male, and voweth, and sacrificeth unto the LORD a corrupt thing: for I am a great King, saith the LORD of hosts, and my name is dreadful among the heathen.

4. <u>MATTHEW 6:7</u>

But when ye pray, use not vain repetitions, as the heathen do: for they think that they shall be heard for their much speaking.

5. <u>2 KINGS 17:15</u>

And they rejected his statutes, and his covenant that he made with their fathers, and his testimonies which he testified against them; and they followed vanity, and became vain, and went after the heathen that were round about them, concerning whom the LORD had charged them, that they should not do like them.

6. <u>PSALMS 47:8</u>

God reigneth over the heathen: God sitteth upon the throne of his holiness.

PURE THOUGHTS & ACTIONS

"Unto the pure all things are pure: but unto them
that are defiled and unbelieving is nothing pure; but even
their mind and conscience is defiled."
Titus 1:15 KJV

Everyone is accountable for the things they do and say. Generally, this is a manifestation of what the mind has conceived. Christ requires those who have clean hands and pure hearts to worship him. Genuine worshippers must approach the Father believing that He is the omnipotent, omniscient, omnipresent God. We should never doubt God's nature or His ability to do more than we can conceive in our limited minds. If we try to relate to God only as a man, we would generally have a defiled view of who God is, therefore, we would never be able to see Him as God.

If we understand Him as the only true God who cannot lie and does not change, our thoughts of God will be pure and undefiled. Understand if we doubt God it would not be because of who He is, but because of who we are. We would have been defiled because we have mixed ourselves with the heathen of this world and have allowed their ideas and their ideologies to make us impure. When we speak of the mark of the beast, we recognise that it is not a chip, but the choices we make and the actions we take that indicate we have been defiled in mind and conscience.

Let us seek to have pure thoughts and clean hands that will allow us to believe God's word unto our own salvation. Wherewithal shall a young man cleanse his way? By taking heed thereto according to Thy word.

WEEKLY WEAPON: <u>I shall purify my mind and not be defiled.</u>

1. **1 JOHN 3:3**

   Wherewithal shall a young man cleanse his way? by taking
   heed thereto according to thy word

2. **1 PETER 1:22**

   Seeing ye have purified your souls in obeying the truth
   through the Spirit unto unfeigned love of the brethren, see that
   ye love one another with a pure heart fervently:

3. **JAMES 1:27**

   Pure religion and undefiled before God and the Father is this,
   To visit the fatherless and widows in their affliction, and to
   keep himself unspotted from the world.

4. **PHILIPPIANS 4:8**

   Finally, brethren, whatsoever things are true, whatsoever
   things are honest, whatsoever things are just, whatsoever
   things are pure, whatsoever things are lovely, whatsoever
   things are of good report; if there be any virtue, and if there be
   any praise, think on these things.

5. **PSALMS 119: 1**

   Blessed are the undefiled   in the way, who walk in the law of
   the LORD.

6. **1 Timothy 1:5**

   Now the end of the commandment is charity out of
   a pure heart, and of a good conscience, and of faith unfeigned:

STEPHEN STONED FOR TRUTH

"And said, Behold, I see the heavens opened, and
the Son of man standing on the right hand of God."
Acts 7:56 KJV

The story of Stephen is worth a revisit, especially today, in these times of upheavals. Stephen, one of the first deacons of the church, was full of the Holy Ghost; honest and full of wisdom i.e. he had a deep reverence for God. Because he was filled with the Spirit and preached in and out of season he was taken before the Jewish council. Stephen calmly and clearly spoke of the scriptures in such a way that no one could refute him because he stayed within the word. He had studied the word and spoke such precious truth, following the historical timeline of God's people.

It was when Stephen touched on present truth, the current state of affairs of the Jewish people and Christ's position in heaven that the council decided to stone him. Stephen said Christ was 'standing". The Jews knew that when God is described as standing, this meant that judgement was pronounced. The angel Gabriel, speaking of the end of time, told Daniel in Daniel 12, 'and at that time shall Michael stand up' and the people shall be delivered. The signs of these times tell us that Christ is about to stand up again and God's people are not ready.

How are we standing today? Are we on the Lord's side or are we gathering stones to kill the messages in God's word? We gather stones to kill the word when we refuse to study the word, when we refuse to pray and commit ourselves to being obedient to the word of God. Let us become acquainted with the truth- preach it in and out of season and be ready to receive Christ as our Saviour.

WEEKLY WEAPON: <u>I stand ready to be stoned for God's word.</u>

1. <u>2 CORINTHIANS 12:10</u>

   Therefore I take pleasure in infirmities, in reproaches, in necessities, in persecutions, in distresses for Christ's sake: for when I am weak, then am I strong.

2. <u>3 JOHN 1:4</u>

   I have no greater joy than to hear that my children walk in truth.

3. <u>1 JOHN 2:4</u>

   He that saith, I know him, and keepeth not his commandments, is a liar, and the truth is not in him.

4. <u>1 JOHN 4:6</u>

   We are of God: he that knoweth God heareth us; he that is not of God heareth not us. Hereby know we the spirit of truth, and the spirit of error.

5. <u>PHILIPPIANS 1:27</u>

   Only let your conversation be as it becometh the gospel of Christ: that whether I come and see you, or else be absent, I may hear of your affairs, that ye stand fast in one spirit, with one mind striving together for the faith of the gospel;

6. <u>DANIEL 12:1</u>

   And at that time shall Michael stand up, the great prince which standeth for the children of thy people: and there shall be a time of trouble, such as never was since there was a nation even to that same time: and at that time thy people shall be delivered, every one that shall be found written in the book.

I WILL TAKE HIS NAME

"And in that day seven women shall take hold of one man, saying, We will eat our own bread, and wear our own apparel: only let us be called by thy name, to take away our reproach."
Isaiah 4:1 KJV

Today, we see the fulfilment of this prophecy of Isaiah. There are so many groups (churches) who seek to be called followers of Christ but do their own thing.

Not because a group of people who come together using some teachings of Christ mixed with their own customs and traditions mean they are Christ's bride. His bride will be a group of law abiding, obedient, believers who look like, sound like and behave like Christ. It will not be a name association but a character affiliation that will identify the true church.

This church will comprise men, women, Jew and gentile, bond and free but they will be of one faith and have the character of Jesus. Such a church will be different from the world; it will be a peculiar group whose leader is Christ and no one else. This group will not frown on being perfect, but will embrace it as a life's journey.

Today, let us seek to have our membership moved to this church. This church studies the word and answers to just one leader- Jesus Christ.

WEEKLY WEAPON: <u>I shall be a member of the Lord's army</u>

<u>POWER TEXTS FOR THE WEEK</u>

1. <u>MATTHEW 7:21</u>

Not every one that saith unto me, Lord, Lord, shall enter into the kingdom of heaven; but he that doeth the will of my Father which is in heaven.

2. <u>REVELATION 12:17</u>

And the dragon was wroth with the woman, and went to make war with the remnant of her seed, which keep the commandments of God, and have the testimony of Jesus Christ.

3. <u>Revelation 2:17</u>

He that hath an ear, let him hear what the Spirit saith unto the churches; To him that overcometh will I give to eat of the hidden manna, and will give him a white stone, and in the stone a new name written, which no man knoweth saving he that receiveth it.

4. <u>GALATIANS 3:28</u>

There is neither Jew nor Greek, there is neither bond nor free, there is neither male nor female: for ye are all one in Christ Jesus.

5. <u>HEBREWS 6:12</u>

That ye be not slothful, but followers of them who through faith and patience inherit the promises.

6. <u>PHILIPPIANS 3:15</u>

Let us therefore, as many as be perfect, be thus minded: and if in any thing ye be otherwise minded, God shall reveal even this unto you.

978 976 96110 4 7